The ONE YEAR BIBLE

GOD SIGHTINGS™
LEARNING TO EXPERIENCE GOD EVERY DAY™

SMALL GROUP LEADER GUIDE

Group
Loveland, Colorado
group.com

Group resources actually work!

This Group resource incorporates our R.E.A.L. approach to ministry. It reinforces a growing friendship with Jesus, encourages long-term learning, and results in life transformation, because it's

Relational
Learner-to-learner interaction enhances learning and builds Christian friendships.

Experiential
What learners experience through discussion and action sticks with them up to 9 times longer than what they simply hear or read.

Applicable
The aim of Christian education is to equip learners to be both hearers and doers of God's Word.

Learner-based
Learners understand and retain more when the learning process takes into consideration how they learn best.

GOD SIGHTINGS™
Learning to Experience God Every Day™
THE ONE YEAR SMALL GROUP LEADER GUIDE

Visit our website: **group.com**

Credits
Contributing Authors: Stephanie Caro, Linda Crawford, Bob D'Ambrosio, Kate S. Holburn, Mikal Keefer, Jan Kershner, Kristi Rector, Siv M. Ricketts, Larry Shallenberger, Carl Simmons, Kelli B. Trujillo, Amber Van Schooneveld, Vicki L.O. Witte, Jill Wuellner
Senior Editor: Candace McMahan
Editors: Linda Crawford and Jill Wuellner
Chief Creative Officer: Joani Schultz
Art Director: Paul Povolni
Cover Designer: Holly Voget
Book Designers: Holly Voget and Jean Bruns
Print Production: Paragon Prepress
Production Manager: Peggy Naylor

Unless otherwise indicated, all Scripture quotations are taken from the *Holy Bible*, New Living Translation, copyright © 1996, 2004, 2007. Used by permission of Tyndale House Publishers, Inc., Carol Stream, Illinois 60188. All rights reserved.

ISBN: 978-0-7644-3926-1

10 9 8 7 6 5 4 3 2 1   18 17 16 15 14 13 12 11 10 09

Printed in Canada.

Welcome to God Sightings™ Small Groups

Connect the dots...between God and life.

Amazing things happen when people explore the Bible every day *and* begin to look for God in the world around them. They detect God in the smile of a passing stranger. The song of a bird on a chilly morning. Conversations with friends.

When people recognize God's participation in their everyday lives, their faith becomes relevant. Vibrant. Thrilling.

And they want to share it.

That's where God Sightings small groups come in.

God Sightings sessions are different.

Yes, they're thought-provoking. They're interactive. And they're fun.

But most important, they encourage people to talk about how God showed up in their lives each week.

In fact, each session begins by asking people to share their God Sightings. It's quite possible that your group will spend entire get-togethers just doing that. And that will do more to draw them closer to Jesus and one another than anything else they could do!

You don't have to "cover the material" in these sessions.

These sessions are meant to be organic, spontaneous, and centered on God. How God has revealed himself through the circumstances of everyday life. And what that means to his followers.

So you won't have to painstakingly research Bible passages or prepare a lesson. In fact, you'll have to do very little in the way of preparation. (Thumb through this book, and take a look at the "Before You Gather" section at the beginning of each week to see for yourself.)

Your group members don't have to prepare, either.

The sessions don't depend on the people in your small group doing all the readings in *God Sightings™: The One Year Bible* each week. In fact, you'll want to encourage them to join in the discussion even when they've taken a break from daily Bible reading.

Someone jokingly said, "This is the guilt-free Bible-reading plan. I like that!" And in the same breath, he said, "I can't believe how active God has been in my life; I just never stopped to notice or give God credit before. Being on the lookout for God Sightings and reading God's Word has really helped me see God."

So when someone in your group shares an especially meaningful God Sighting, ask if you can tell your pastor so that everyone in your church can hear about it. Excitement surrounding God Sightings is contagious!

Just remember, people can start their Bible-reading programs, stop, and resume at any time without ever missing a get-together with the group. And the entire group can decide to take a break, too... during holidays, summer vacation, all those superbusy times of life that have derailed so many of us who want to explore God's Word every day.

Here's the thing: Life happens. But God keeps showing up. Encourage all the people in your small group to open their eyes to God's presence in the midst of life.

May God bless you and your small group as you learn to experience God every day!

Expect the Unexpected

Before you gather:
Place coffee filters (1 for every four or five people), paper, and pens on a table.

Learning to Experience God Every Day

Welcome everyone. Describe one way you experienced God this week. Then say something like: **This year as we read through the Bible, God will become more real to us than ever. We will see God in fresh, new ways every day—if we open our eyes to see him.** Ask each person to tell about a God Sighting that happened this week.

Go!

Form groups of four or five, and give each group a coffee filter, paper, and a pen. Tell groups they'll have five minutes to brainstorm 10 alternative uses (other than for making coffee) for a coffee filter. After five minutes have elapsed, encourage groups to share their answers. Here are some examples of alternative uses for coffee filters:

• to apply shoe polish

• as a lint-free way to clean mirrors and windows

• as a food holder for messy tacos or cookies

• to line flowerpots to keep soil from falling through the drainage holes

Have each group discuss:

❧This activity challenged you to take a different look at a commonplace item. Do you regularly challenge yourself to view everyday things in different ways? Why or why not?

❧WEEK 1—January 1-7

Genesis 1:1–18:15; Matthew 1:1–6:24;
Psalms 1–7; Proverbs 1:1–2:5

Go Deeper

Form smaller groups of three or four, and read the following passage from the introduction to *God Sightings: The One Year Companion Guide:*

"**Once you've seen God at work, there's no turning back...You can't wait to see what God will do next. Because—maybe for the first time—you see him *alive and active* in your world...It's one thing to master the Bible—to know about God and his history with his creation. It's great information, a rock-solid foundation.**

"**But to *experience* God in a fresh, powerful way?**

"**That's life itself.**"

Next, ask group members to reflect on the quote and the activity they just completed as they discuss:

❧**How can having "everyday" expectations of God influence your ability to see what God is doing in your life?**

Call everyone together, and share highlights from the discussions.

Go Forward

Say: **Scientific experiments have shown that *what we see is often affected by what we expect to see.* Before our meeting, we looked at coffee filters and saw them only as coffee filters. Perhaps when we've looked at God, we've also seen only what we expected to see.**

Ask people to think of a situation in their lives in which they desire to see God alive and active. Then discuss:

❧**How can you change your perception or expectations so you'll see more of God's presence in this situation?**

Ask a volunteer to read Matthew 5:8. Pray together, asking God to give you pure hearts and eyes and minds that are open to see God at work in fresh, new ways. Pray for participants to see God over the next week as they pray and read the Bible, as well as during everyday life—on the drive to work, in a child's laugh, through the generosity of a friend, and more!

Promises You Can Bank On

Before you gather:

Photocopy the Week 2 handout, "Some Promises From God," at the end of this guide. You'll need a promise for each person. Cut the promises into individual strips, fold the strips, and place them in a basket or bowl.

Learning to Experience God Every Day

Welcome everyone. Ask each person to tell about a God Sighting that happened this week.

Go!

After everyone has had a chance to share, ask people to find a partner and follow these instructions:

1. **Find an item you have with you that's valuable or important to you—a wedding ring, cell phone, car or house key, wallet, or eyeglasses, for example.**

2. **Give that item to your partner.**

3. **If you're the first person to receive, say nothing. If you're the second person to receive, look the giver in the eye and say, "I promise to keep this in a safe place and to give it back to you when you need it."**

After pairs have exchanged items, gather everyone to discuss:

❧ **How did you feel when you had to give something important to another person?**

❧ **What did you think when the person who received it said nothing?**

❧ **If you received a promise, how did the promise make you feel?**

❧ **WEEK 2—January 8-14**

Genesis 18:16–31:16; Matthew 6:25–10:23;
Psalms 8–12; Proverbs 2:6–3:15

Go Deeper

Form groups of three or four, and ask people to take turns in their groups sharing responses to these questions:

- ❧**Describe a time you had to entrust something important to someone else's care. How did you feel? How did things turn out?**

- ❧**How are the promises people make and the promises God makes different?**

Go Forward

Gather everyone, and ask people to return the items given to them earlier.

Read one of the first and most extravagant promises from God in the Bible: Genesis 26:4. Now ask everyone to silently reflect on the character of a God who can make such astonishing promises—and keep them! Ask people to identify something in their own lives that reveals God's promises to them. Is it a sunrise? a smile? a special gift? a "regular" God Sighting?

After one or two minutes, ask people to think of something in their lives or hearts they need to entrust to God. Before they share, have everyone take a Scripture promise from the basket or bowl.

Ask people to each read the promise from God's Word and share how it will help them trust God in the coming week.

After everyone has read a promise, pray together, praising God for fulfilling his promises and asking him to help you trust him fully throughout the coming week.

Some *Promises* From God

- God will always love you (Romans 8:35-39).
- God will always forgive you (1 John 1:9).
- God will provide direction for your life (Proverbs 3:5-6).
- God will hear and answer your prayers (Proverbs 15:29 and 1 John 5:14).
- God will always be with you (Isaiah 41:10 and Matthew 28:20).
- God will enable you to face temptation (1 Corinthians 10:13).
- God will meet your needs (Matthew 6:25-33).

Booked Up?

....

Before you gather:
Encourage people to bring their own calendars, phones, or PDAs to the meeting. Be sure to bring one yourself!

....

Learning to Experience God Every Day

Welcome everyone. Ask each person to tell about a God Sighting that happened this week.

Go!

After everyone has had a chance to share, ask people to use both hands to hold their phones, PDAs, or planners out in front of them. As they hold their hands outstretched, ask people to take turns describing the past week and what their phones or planning devices reveal about how burdened, stressed-out, or busy they were. After everyone has shared, allow people to lower their arms, set aside their phones and planners, and discuss:

❧**How do busy schedules help or hinder God Sightings?**

❧**WEEK 3—January 15-21**

Genesis 31:17—43:34; Matthew 10:24—14:12;
Psalms 13:1—18:36; Proverbs 3:16—4:10

Go Deeper

Ask a volunteer to read aloud Matthew 11:28-30. Discuss:

&Outer circumstances may not change, but your inner posture can. In your experience, what's the difference between carrying your own burdens and resting in Jesus? How does it *feel* to rest in Jesus? How does that compare to how it felt to relax your arms and set your phone or planner aside?

Go Forward

Have everyone form pairs and discuss:

&Some stressors are beyond your control. But what about causes of stress that you *can* control? What, specifically, might God be calling you to change?

Encourage partners to share with each other one specific action they'll take to prioritize time so they can truly rest in Jesus. Then ask group members to pick up their planning devices and schedule a time to do this during the coming week.

Finally, prompt partners to pray together, holding out their planners as symbols of their willingness to surrender their burdens to Jesus.

Satisfied

....

Before you gather:
Spoon individual servings of whipped cream into small bowls, and assemble a plate of assorted fruit, nuts, cheese, and crackers to snack on later. Have spoons, pens, and paper available.

....

Learning to Experience God Every Day

Welcome everyone. Ask each person to tell about a God Sighting that happened this week.

Go!

After everyone has had a chance to share, offer everyone a bowl of whipped cream to enjoy as you discuss these questions:

🎝 **If you were a food critic, how would you describe the positive aspects of serving whipped cream as a snack food? What are its negative aspects?**

🎝 **At home or in a restaurant, would you eat a bowl of whipped cream for dessert? Why or why not?**

Form groups of three or four, and discuss:

🎝 **Describe an example from this past week of expecting to receive one thing but getting whipped cream instead! Was it a positive or negative experience?**

🎝 **WEEK 4—January 22-28**

Genesis 44:1–Exodus 7:25; Matthew 14:13–19:12;
Psalms 18:37–23:6; Proverbs 4:11–5:23

Go Deeper

Make sure each group has a sheet of paper and a pen. Ask each group to make a four-column list with these headings: "Appetizers," "Main Courses," "Desserts," and "Snacks." Next ask groups to list current *needs* in the appropriate categories. For example, a need for fun and laughter could go under "Desserts," a need for a job under "Main Courses," and a need for God under all four headings!

After the groups have completed their lists, ask them to read Psalm 23:1 and discuss:

❧ **In this verse, God promises to provide all that we need. How can giving us whipped cream instead of a steak meet a need?**

❧ **How are our *wants* and *needs* different? similar?**

❧ **How have you tried to satisfy your wants this week instead of asking God to give you what you need?**

Go Forward

Gather the entire group, offer the plate of healthy snack foods for everyone to enjoy, and discuss:

❧ **How is this food more satisfying than the whipped cream?**

❧ **Just looking at food on a plate won't satisfy hunger. What actions must we take to satisfy hunger?**

❧ **What must we do to receive nourishment from Scripture?**

Read Psalm 23, and encourage participants to consider the words as food for their souls. Ask them to try to see God in a new way during their reading time this week—and to share a wonderful meal with him! Close with prayer, asking God to help all of you turn to him as the only true satisfaction for your deepest needs.

What's Love Got to Do With It?

Before you gather:

Photocopy the Week 5 handout, "Mind Challenge," at the end of this guide. You'll need one copy for each group of three or four.

Learning to Experience God Every Day

Welcome everyone. Ask each person to tell about a God Sighting that happened this week.

Go!

After everyone has had a chance to share, form groups of three or four, give each group a copy of "Mind Challenge," and give groups five minutes to find a solution to the challenge. Call everyone together to share answers. If no one discovered the correct answer, provide the solution and the reasoning behind it. Discuss:

❧How do you feel when you're faced with challenges that confound you?

❧How was this experience similar to reading a command in Scripture that you're not sure how to respond to?

Go Deeper

Ask a volunteer to read Matthew 22:37. Form groups of three or four to discuss:

❧The "Mind Challenge" required you to use your mind to analyze the issue and apply logic to discover the solution. How do we use our minds in a similar way to discover God's truth? to love God?

❧**WEEK 5—January 29–February 4**

Exodus 8:1–21:21; Matthew 19:13–23:39;
Psalms 24–28; Proverbs 6:1–7:5

✎The door dilemma challenged your mind primarily. What real-life dilemmas challenge your mind? your heart? your soul?

✎Why does God require us to love him with more than just our hearts? How will loving God with our hearts, souls, and minds help us choose the right doors in life?

Go Forward

Gather everyone to share highlights from group discussions. Be sure to recognize any God Sightings—glimpses of God at work in people's hearts, souls, and minds during your time together. Discuss:

✎Jesus didn't say "some" or "most"; he said "all." Love with *all* your heart, soul, and mind. That's a tall order! It may be a challenge when we're not sure exactly how to do that. So how *do* we do it?

Ask people to identify one aspect (heart, soul, or mind) of their love for God that they want to focus on this week and to share how they will give more of it to God!

Conclude with a silent group prayer. Tell participants that you'd like them to each individually express love to God; you'll guide the prayer by directing the group's focus. Pray something like this:

Lord, I love you with all my heart...(*Allow time for silent prayer.*)

Lord, I love you with all my soul...(*Allow time for silent prayer.*)

Lord, I love you with all my mind...(*Allow time for silent prayer.*)

Teach us how to love you more deeply every day. In Jesus' name, amen.

Mind Challenge

You are trapped in a room with two doors. One leads to certain death, and the other leads to freedom. You don't know which is which.

There are two people guarding the doors. You can choose one door, and then you must go through it.

You may ask either guard one question. The problem is, one guard always tells the truth and the other always lies. You don't know which is which.

What is the right question to ask?

Solution: Ask one guard what the other guard would say if he were asked which door was safe. Then go through the other door.

Jesus in Disguise

Before you gather:
Find at least one item of old, worn-out clothing, such as a torn and dirty jacket.

Learning to Experience God Every Day

Welcome everyone. Ask each person to tell about a God Sighting that happened this week.

Go!

After everyone has had a chance to share, ask the group to sit in a circle. Show the group the item of worn, dirty clothing.

Pass the item around the circle, and as people hold it, invite them each to share one word that describes how holding it makes them feel. (Disgusted? Uncomfortable? Sad?)

Ask a volunteer to put the garment on over his or her own clothes, and then ask:

❧**How does it change [name's] appearance? How could it change your first impression of who [he or she] is?**

Go Deeper

Form groups of three or four, and read this quote from Mother Teresa:

"We try to pray through our work by doing it with Jesus, for Jesus, to Jesus. That helps us put our whole heart and soul into doing it. The dying, the crippled, the mentally ill, the unwanted, the unloved—they are Jesus in disguise."

❧**Week 6—February 5-11**

Exodus 21:22–33:23; Matthew 24:1–27:14;
Psalms 29:1–33:11; Proverbs 7:6–8:36

- How did the worn clothing disguise [name]? How could a homeless person be "Jesus in disguise"?

- Have you ever tried to view people as Jesus in disguise? What makes it difficult? easy?

Invite a volunteer to read Matthew 25:31-40; then discuss:

- Jesus said that whatever is done to the weak and outcast is done to him. Who did you see, drive past, or interact with this week who would fit the description of someone outcast, someone unloved, someone in need? How did you respond?

- Imagine someone here on earth truly *was* Jesus but in the disguise of an ailing, homeless person on a street corner. How can we change our thinking to see that person as a God Sighting instead of a homeless person?

Go Forward

In the same groups of four, discuss:

- Who do you feel God is calling you to treat as if that person were Jesus in disguise? Why?

- How do you feel compelled to act toward that individual or group of people?

Ask everyone to sit in one big circle. Pass the worn garment around the circle again. As people hold it, invite them each to share the specific action or attitude change they feel God is developing in their hearts toward people in need.

Then pray together, with the item of clothing in the middle of the circle, inviting God to give you fresh eyes to see Jesus in the poor, unwanted, and lost people you encounter.

Ready, Set, Go Teach!

Learning to Experience God Every Day

Welcome everyone. Ask each person to tell about a God Sighting that happened this week.

Go!

After everyone has had a chance to share, ask each person to answer this question:

> ❧What's something you know how to do that you would be confident teaching to someone else?

Take the time to listen and learn about one another's talents and interests. Then ask people to form pairs or trios and to briefly describe how they would teach their skills or talents. What approach or steps would they take?

Go Deeper

Ask pairs (or trios) to join another pair to discuss:

> ❧Name one teacher or person who taught you something that made a difference in your life. What did he or she teach you? How did you see God in that person?

❧**Week 7—February 12-18**

Exodus 34:1–Leviticus 7:27; Matthew 27:15–
Mark 3:30; Psalms 33:12–37:11; Proverbs 9:1–10:4

Ask a volunteer to read Jesus' final charge to his followers in Matthew 28:18-20, and continue your discussion:

❧ Are you as confident about your ability to teach about Jesus as you are about your ability to teach the skill you shared? Why or why not?

❧ What experiences in your life have taught you the most about your faith? How can sharing these experiences help you teach others about Jesus?

Go Forward

Ask people to stay in the same small groups and think about the past week as they discuss:

❧ What opportunities did God give you to live out Jesus' call to make disciples? (Think of opportunities you took advantage of, as well as opportunities you might have missed.)

❧ Who do you feel God might want you to invite to follow Jesus? Whose spiritual growth might God want you to encourage?

After everyone has shared, lead the group to pray by name for each person mentioned and for one another, asking God to give them the courage to live out Jesus' challenge to live as disciples and to make disciples.

Encourage members to recognize Jesus as their teacher as they share their faith during the coming week.

How Long Will You Wait?

Before you gather:

Number small slips of paper from 1 up to the number of people in your group. Write "1" on additional slips of paper so you can give one to each person at the closing. You'll need the song "40" by U2 and a way to play it. (You may find it on iTunes, Rhapsody.com, or U2's album *Under a Blood Red Sky.*)

Learning to Experience God Every Day

Welcome everyone. Ask each person to tell about a God Sighting that happened this week.

Go!

After everyone has had a chance to share, have each person "take a number"—a slip of paper with a number on it.

Explain that the numbers people took will be their numbers during discussions. People will share in numerical order, with the lowest numbers always going first. Play the song "40"; then kick off the discussion.

Go Deeper

Form groups of four to six, and have people reveal their numbers so they know in what order they'll answer the discussion questions. Ask people to take turns in their groups as they answer the following questions, with the lowest number going first:

✎**Did you enjoy the song, or was it a test of your patience to listen to it? Why?**

✎**WEEK 8—February 19-25**

Leviticus 7:28–18:30; Mark 3:31–8:10;
Psalms 37:12–41:13; Proverbs 10:5-16

The lyrics keep asking, "How long?" How long can you wait in a line before you start to lose your patience?

Ask a volunteer to read Psalm 40:1-3. Ask people to stay in their groups and answer the following questions in order, according to their numbers.

Think of this passage as song lyrics. How are these lyrics different from the lyrics you listened to earlier? How are they similar?

For the next questions, allow people to share freely, without reference to their numbers:

How did it feel to have to answer the questions in numbered order? How did it feel to have to wait your turn? to always go first?

What if God made us take a number and wait in line before he would listen to and answer our prayers? How well would you wait?

Go Forward

Gather everyone together. Remind people that the song "40" repeats words from Psalm 40 but adds, "How long?" Ask them to turn to a partner to discuss:

What are you asking God "how long" about?

What do you think God wants you to do in your time of waiting?

After 10 minutes, call everyone together and stand in the center or in front of the group. Invite people to come to you and exchange their numbered slips of paper for new ones. Give everyone a number 1.

Remind people that in God's kingdom, everyone has immediate access to God's presence and love. Encourage them to look for evidence of God in their times of waiting in the coming week. Close your time together by rephrasing Psalm 40:1-3 in a prayer of thanksgiving.

Recess Time!

....

Before you gather:
Choose one of your favorite childhood games that everyone in your group can play. (It may be an indoor or outdoor game, depending on your climate; see the suggestions on the next page.)

....

Learning to Experience God Every Day

Welcome everyone. Ask each person to tell about a God Sighting that happened this week.

Go!

After everyone has had a chance to share, explain that you're all going to play one of your favorite childhood games. Maybe others will tell about their favorites and challenge the group to play them for a few minutes. Agree on a game, and begin!

Go Deeper

Allow people to play for about 20 minutes; then ask them to form groups of three or four and discuss:

෯What did you enjoy most about this recess time?

෯Why do you think recess is usually a child's favorite part of the school day?

෯As an adult, how often do you take a recess from your busy life? Why is it more difficult as an adult to make time to just play?

෯WEEK 9—February 26–March 4

Leviticus 19–Numbers 3; Mark 8:11–12:17;
Psalms 42–47; Proverbs 10:17-25

After about 10 minutes of discussion, call everyone together. Ask people to share highlights of their time spent in play and discussion. Then ask each person to turn to a partner and complete this sentence:

"I saw God in _____ during our recess time." (Our laughter? Smiles? Silliness? Joy?)

Go Forward

Say: **Kids love to play, are curious, and have a simple faith. What's one childlike quality you would like to have more of in your life?**

Read Mark 10:15, and ask everyone to discuss:

❧**At heart, our faith is simple, one that even a child can embrace. How can you be more childlike in your approach to God this week?**

❧**How can more joy and laughter help you see more of God?**

Close in prayer, thanking God for requiring only a simple, childlike faith. Ask God to help people take time out for recess during the coming week and look for more God Sightings in the laughter and smiles of the people around them.

Indoor Games

Candy Land, Sorry!, Twister, Trivial Pursuit, Jenga, Bop It, Monopoly, Guesstures

Outdoor Games

badminton, croquet, relay races, volleyball, giant bubbles, Hula-Hoops, horseshoes

Recycled and Renewed

Before you gather:

Gather several items that can be recycled, such as used newspapers, aluminum cans, or water bottles. Have pens available. On a large sheet of paper, write these definitions of *recycling*, and display it for all to see:

- Processing used materials into new products
- Reconditioning and adapting to a new use or function
- Capable of being used again
- Saving from loss and restoring to usefulness

Learning to Experience God Every Day

Welcome everyone. Ask each person to tell about a God Sighting that happened this week.

Go!

After everyone has had a chance to share, display a few recyclable items. In pairs, discuss:

❧What aspects of recycling appeal to you? What isn't so appealing? Why?

Go Deeper

Form slightly larger groups of four or five. Using the definitions of *recycling* you posted, discuss:

❧Share how God has recycled one of your mistakes or sins and reconditioned you for a new use or function.

❧How has God saved you from self-condemnation and despair and restored you to usefulness?

❧**WEEK 10—March 5-11**

Numbers 4:1–16:40; Mark 12:18–15:47;
Psalms 48-54; Proverbs 10:26–11:6

❧What is your role and responsibility in the recycling and renewing process God works in you?

Go Forward

Gather the group, and tear the paper with the recycling definitions into pieces so everyone in the group has a piece. Ask people to use the paper to write their answers to this question:

❧What one thing would you like to give to God this week to recycle or renew in your life?

Ask people to recycle their pieces of paper into bookmarks to use during their Bible readings in the next week. Remind them to look for God Sightings in the recycling and renewing processes God is working in their lives!

Close your time together by praying the words of Psalm 51:10-12 and by asking God to recycle and renew your hearts and spirits so you can sense more of his presence in your lives.

Bonus Idea

If your group would like to do a simple recycling project together, check out these ideas:

• **Used athletic shoes** can be recycled into playground surfaces. See nikereuseashoe.com.

• **Clothing** may be donated to shelters, the Red Cross, local charities, or families in need in your community.

• **Books and magazines** may be donated to local libraries, shelters, schools, hospitals, and prison ministries.

• **Cell phones and used printer cartridges** may be donated to schools or other charitable organizations that recycle them for money to support their programs.

• **Aluminum cans and glass bottles** may be redeemed for cash. Consider donating the money to a local charity.

• **Newspapers** may be redeemed for cash by some local recycling companies if given in large quantities. Consider donating the cash to a needy charity. Or drop the newspapers in a local recycling bin and save a tree!

• **Unwanted items** may be donated to a charity garage sale or needy families in your community.

The Heart of Worship

Before you gather:

Be prepared to worship! Gather CDs or downloads of your group's favorite worship music. Have slips of paper and pens available.

Learning to Experience God Every Day

Welcome everyone. Ask each person to tell about a God Sighting that happened this week.

Go!

After everyone has had a chance to share, ask people to each make a list of five things from the past week they're thankful for. Form pairs to share lists.

After five minutes, have people gather in a large group and share a few stories of thankfulness they experienced in the last week. Ask people to return to the same pairs to discuss these questions:

❧**In what specific ways do you feel different now, compared with when you first came into our meeting? What caused your feelings to change?**

Go Deeper

After a few minutes, gather the group to share highlights of pairs' discussions. Then ask people to make another list, this time of five qualities of God they're grateful for. Ask people to return to the same pairs to share answers and discuss:

❧**Week 11—March 12-18**

Numbers 16:41–28:15; Mark 16:1–Luke 3:22;
Psalms 55–61; Proverbs 11:7-17

How do your feelings change when you talk about the things you like about God? What thoughts become less important? more important?

What God Sightings did you experience in the last week that led you to praise God for who he is?

Allow 5 to 10 minutes for discussion before gathering the group. Allow time for people to share more God Sightings prompted by their discussions. Ask a volunteer to read the first line of Psalm 57:9, followed by the first line of Psalm 100:4. Ask:

What "gate" opened inside you when you shared what you're thankful for?

Read the second line of Psalm 57:9 and the second line of Psalm 100:4 and discuss:

What "court" do you enter when you praise God for who he is?

Go Forward

Ask members to return to their original pairs and share:

How do you define *worship*?

How much time do you spend each day worshipping God? Is it a priority in your life? Why or why not?

What's one specific thing you will do this week to see more of God's presence in your life?

Encourage members to continue to journal God Sightings and to look for God in the things they are thankful for each day. Close your time together in worship, giving thanks and singing God's praises together.

Inside and Out

Before you gather:

Set these items on a table: tissue paper, gift wrap, ribbons, bows, tape, and scissors. If possible, make the table accessible from both sides. You'll also need a fresh banana peel and a small Bible or devotional book.

Learning to Experience God Every Day

Welcome everyone. Ask each person to tell about a God Sighting that happened this week.

Go!

After everyone has had a chance to share, form two teams, and have them line up assembly-line style on either side of the table. Present one group with a small Bible or devotional book, and give the other a fresh banana peel. Explain that the job for both teams is to wrap the items as beautifully as possible.

When the teams have finished, compare the finished products, and vote on which package is the most beautiful on the *outside*.

✒ WEEK 12—March 19-25

Numbers 28:16–Deuteronomy 4:49; Luke 3:23–7:10; Psalms 62:1–68:18; Proverbs 11:18-28

Go Deeper

Ask members to form groups of three or four and discuss:

- ❧ **Which package best represents how you feel about your-self "inside and out"? Explain.**

- ❧ **If both packages looked equally beautiful on the outside, how could you detect which one had the banana peel in-side? How is this similar to or different from the methods you use to detect what's on the inside of *people*?**

Ask for a volunteer to read Luke 6:45. Discuss:

- ❧ **What words have you said this week that could have come from a "banana peel" heart? How do you feel about what you revealed about your heart through those words?**

- ❧ **Banana peels stink. What words were spoken *to you* this week that have stunk up your life? made it smell better?**

Go Forward

After 10 minutes, gather everyone to share answers to these questions:

- ❧ **How can you detect God Sightings in *words* this week?**

- ❧ **How can you help others see God in you this week?**

Place the two wrapped items in the center of the group. Close in prayer, asking God to make your hearts pure so you will display God's love, in word and in deed, from the inside out.

Rules to Live By

Before you gather:
Have pads of sticky notes and pens available.

Learning to Experience God Every Day

Welcome everyone. Ask each person to tell about a God Sighting that happened this week.

Go!

After everyone has had a chance to share, give each person a small pad of sticky notes and a pen. Instruct people to write as many of the "rules" from their childhood as they can remember in one minute: Don't touch a hot stove, for example. Give each person a chance to share the list of rules with the whole group, and then discuss:

> ❧ **Which of these rules was (or still is) hardest for you to follow? Why?**

> ❧ **Why do you think you still remember these rules?**

Go Deeper

Tell people you have a new rule for them to learn, and ask everyone to write this rule on a sticky note: You may not say the word *I* for the rest of the session. Ask people to think of a strategy that will help them remember the rule.

❧ **WEEK 13—March 26–April 1**

Deuteronomy 5–20; Luke 7:11–9:50;
Psalms 68:19–73:28; Proverbs 11:29–12:10

Form groups of three or four to discuss these questions:

☙**What strategies have you used in the past to help you remember information?**

☙**What strategies do you use to help you remember Scripture? to remember to follow God?**

Read Deuteronomy 6:6-9 together.

☙**How could applying these strategies help you increase the God Sightings in your life?**

Go Forward

After 10 minutes, ask people to share highlights from their discussions. Then review how successful they were in remembering to follow the new rule not to use the word *I*.

☙**Was this rule difficult or easy for you to commit to memory? Why?**

Ask members to silently consider the answer to this question:

☙**God directed the Israelites to commit to his commands. Think about God's personal instructions for your life. What "rule" or instruction have you received from God that you resist?**

Ask people to write whatever God has impressed on their hearts on a new sticky note. Encourage them to take the note home and place it where they'll see it often.

Close your time in prayer, thanking God for loving you enough to give you instructions to live by. Pray that people would see God at work in new ways as they recommit to following his leadership in their lives.

Ask, Seek, Knock

Before you gather:

Photocopy the Week 14 handout, "More Promises From God About…," at the end of the book. You'll need a list for each person.

Learning to Experience God Every Day

Welcome everyone. Ask each person to tell about a God Sighting that happened this week.

Go!

After they've all had a chance to share, ask people to recall something they really, really wanted when they were children. Ask each person to quickly share what he or she wanted and the method the person used to try to get it.

Next ask people to think of something they really *need* in their lives right now. Have them turn to a partner to discuss:

❧ **What methods are you using to ask for what you need right now? How are they similar to or different from the methods you used as a child?**

❧ **WEEK 14—April 2-8**

Deuteronomy 21–32; Luke 9:51–12:59; Psalms 74:1–78:64; Proverbs 12:11-24

Go Deeper

After a few minutes, ask pairs to discuss these questions:

❧ **What helps or hinders your ability to ask God for what you need?**

❧ **What's something you've repeatedly asked God for and haven't yet received? How do you feel about not receiving it yet?**

After 10 minutes, gather the group to share discussion highlights. Ask a volunteer to read Luke 11:9-10. Ask:

❧ **When you pray, do you visualize God on the other side of the door you're knocking on? What about this image appeals to you? repels you?**

Take an informal survey of the group's answers, and then ask people to form groups of four or five to discuss:

❧ **How do you visualize or connect with God when you pray? How can you experience more God Sightings during your prayer time in the next week?**

Go Forward

Give everyone "More Promises From God About…" Ask everyone to find a Scripture (or Scriptures) that contains God's response to the need each person is asking God to address in his or her life right now.

Ask groups of four or five to close in prayer, asking, seeking, and knocking on God's door for each person's need.

Your Money or Your Life?

Before you gather:
Have a watch with a second hand or a stopwatch available, as well as a notepad and pen.

Learning to Experience God Every Day

Welcome everyone. Ask each person to tell about a God Sighting that happened this week.

Go!

After people have shared their God Sightings, ask them to get out their credit cards and all the cash they brought with them. Jot a list of amounts. Gather everyone in a circle, and have people number off by twos. Tell them that when you say "go," they are to throw the currency and cards into the air. Ones will then have 15 seconds to grab as much of it as they can, while Twos just watch.

After 15 seconds, have Ones count the currency and cards they gathered, and name a winner. Leave the currency that wasn't collected where it fell. Ask Ones to pair up with a Two (or form one group of three if you have an uneven number) to discuss these questions:

✎As one of the participants, how would you describe your feelings and behavior during the "money grab"?

✎As a spectator, what was your emotional reaction to witnessing the behavior of the money grabbers?

✎If this had been a game with play money, how do you think your responses would have been different?

> ✎WEEK 15—April 9–15
>
> Deuteronomy 33:1–Joshua 12:24; Luke 13–17;
> Psalms 78:65–84:12; Proverbs 12:25–13:6

Go Deeper

After five minutes of discussion, have each pair join with another pair to form a group of four and discuss:

❧What word would you use to describe how you feel about money and finances in your life right now?

❧Money often tops the list of things couples argue about the most. Do money issues evoke strong emotions in you? Why?

After 10 to 15 minutes of discussion, ask a volunteer to read Luke 16:13. Ask groups to discuss:

❧A 2004 study by the Barna Group revealed that Christians are more likely to buy lottery tickets than non-Christians. Why do you think that's true?

❧How does money sometimes become a "god" in your life? How does it get in the way of loving God? of experiencing God Sightings in financial matters?

Go Forward

Gather in a large circle, and lead everyone in prayer, asking God to help the people in your group release unhealthy feelings or attitudes about money that hinder their relationships with God.

In closing, ask people to—one at a time—throw the money into a pile in the middle of the group. Ask everyone to accompany the action with a verbal commitment similar to this: "In my life, I choose to serve and love God, not money." After all the currency is in a pile, pray for God to shift your group's focus off money issues and onto God, so all can see and experience God's presence—especially in financial matters—in fresh, new ways in the coming weeks.

Return the money to the owners.

Who Will You Serve?

Learning to Experience God Every Day

Welcome everyone. Ask each person to tell about a God Sighting that happened this week.

Go!

After everyone has had a chance to share, ask people to take part in a test of skill. Tell them to remain seated and "draw" circles by moving their right feet clockwise. Then tell them to continue moving their right feet in clockwise circles as they draw the number 6 in the air with their right index fingers.

Allow several minutes for people to attempt to follow the instructions; then ask everyone to turn to a partner and discuss:

❧**During the activity your foot was going in the "right" direction until the movement of your hand influenced it. How is this experience like or unlike trying to follow God's direction for your life?**

Allow time for pairs to share their answers briefly with the large group.

Go Deeper

Have pairs discuss:

❧**Describe a challenge in your life right now that pulls you in two different directions.**

Ask a volunteer to read Joshua 24:15. Ask pairs to discuss:

❧**What things in your life test your commitment to serving God and following his direction for your life?**

Go Forward

Gather everyone, and discuss:

❧**How can choosing to serve God in the midst of challenges to your faith help you catch more glimpses of God?**

❧**What attitudes or perceptions do you need to work on in order to be less influenced by those around you and better equipped to follow God's direction for your life?**

Have pairs get together one more time to share and commit to a practical step they'll take this week to place a higher priority on serving God. Pray for closer fellowship with God and the ability to see God working through them as they choose to serve God and follow his direction for their lives. To close, ask each person to pray aloud the last sentence of Joshua 24:15.

Not My Will

Before you gather:
Make arrangements to play soft worship music at the end of your meeting.

Learning to Experience God Every Day

Welcome everyone. Ask each person to tell about a God Sighting that happened this week.

Go!

After everyone has had a chance to share, ask people to imagine what their lives would be like if they had everything they want: the perfect job, perfect family, perfect personality—perfect everything! Have people turn to partners and describe their perfect lives. Encourage them to have fun with their ideas but to be honest, too!

After partners have shared, have them each introduce their "perfected" friend and describe his or her new life to the group. Then ask pairs to discuss:

❧How different is your fantasy self from your real self?

❧If you could really change things so life was easy and "perfect," do you think you would be happier? Why or why not?

❧**WEEK 17—April 23-29**

Judges 1–10; Luke 21:29–24:53;
Psalms 90–100; Proverbs 13:24–14:12

Go Deeper

Allow about 10 minutes for discussion, and then read
Luke 22:41-42. Discuss in small groups of three or four:

❧In our fantasy lives, we can imagine away suffering and
hardship. But what was Jesus' response to suffering in
this Scripture?

❧How do you respond when you're suffering or struggling
with difficulties?

After about 10 minutes, invite volunteers to share highlights from
their discussion with the whole group.

Go Forward

Ask people to return to their partners and discuss:

❧What God Sighting have you had during a difficult time
in the past that can help you follow God's will for your
life now—no matter how hard it is?

❧What situation are you facing in which you don't know
God's will?

To end your time together, play soft worship music, and invite
people to spread out around your meeting space—so they won't
be easily distracted—and spend a few minutes privately talking
with God. Encourage them to ask God to help them let go of
their fantasy desires and surrender their hearts and minds to
God's will rather than their own.

For God So Loved...

Before you gather:
Use a utility knife to cut through the binding of an old phone book. Cut the phone book into sections, each with several pages of names, so you have one for each person.

Learning to Experience God Every Day

Welcome everyone. Ask each person to tell about a God Sighting that happened this week.

Go!

After everyone has had a chance to share, give each person a phone-book section. Instruct people to look through the names and memorize as many as they can in one minute.

After one minute, have the group form pairs. As one partner listens and counts, the other partner will recite the names he or she memorized. Then have partners switch roles.

Ask partners to take turns reciting as many names of personal friends as they can in 30 seconds while the other person counts.

Finally, ask them to recite the names of all the people they love deeply as their partners count the names.

Call the group together, and ask people to share their numbers. How many names from the phone book did people memorize? How many friends were named? How many dearly loved people were named?

Go Deeper

Ask people to tear their phone books into smaller pieces and make a large pile of pieces in the center of the group. (Explain that the phone books will go into a recycling bin at the end of the meeting; people can tear them up as much as they want.)

Say: **Look at the pile of torn-up names. What kinds of things tear people up in real life?**

After a few minutes, tell members they now have one minute to put the pieces back together! Acknowledge how ridiculous your request is, and say something like: **Of course you can't put these pieces back together, so they're still going to be thrown away...unless you can think of a way to give them a new purpose or life.**

Allow the group two minutes to brainstorm ways to give the pile of torn-up pages a new purpose.

Go Forward

After brainstorming, ask a volunteer to read John 3:16. Ask people to work together to arrange the torn pages into the shape of a cross. After they've completed the cross, discuss:

✎**How does it feel to look at all of these torn names?**

✎**How can you see God in this pile of torn names?**

✎**How can this image help you see and feel more of God's love for the world? for you?**

Close by asking people to place their hands on the torn pages and pray for the people God loves—all the people of the world. Pray that those known to you and those you don't know—*all* of whom are known and loved by God—will catch sight of the God who loves them so much he sacrificed his only Son for them.

Blessed Are Those Who Hunger

Before you gather:

Set out paper plates and cups. Provide a marker or pen for each person. (Optional: Download the song "Blessed Are Those Who Hunger" by Tom Ewing on iTunes or Rhapsody.com, or obtain a copy of Tom Ewing's CD *The Now and Then* to play at the end of your meeting as everyone prays silently.)

Learning to Experience God Every Day

Welcome everyone. Ask each person to tell about a God Sighting that happened this week.

Go!

After everyone has had a chance to share, invite people to enjoy a "feast of the Word" by choosing a favorite Scripture verse or verses from past weeks' readings. Then ask them to copy the Scripture references onto their plates or cups and indicate which part of the meal the Scriptures represent to them.

Ask members to form groups of four or five to discuss:

❧**What Scripture "food" choices did you make? Why did you choose each one to be that particular part of your "meal"? How does Scripture feed and nourish you?**

❧**WEEK 19—May 7-13**

1 Samuel 1–14; John 5–7; Psalms
105:37–109:31; Proverbs 14:28–15:7

Go Deeper

Gather the entire group, and ask a volunteer to read John 6:35 and Matthew 6:11. Have everyone return to the smaller groups to discuss:

❧Jesus promises that if we come to him, we will never be hungry again. What kind of hunger does Jesus satisfy? How has he satisfied that hunger in you this week?

❧Jesus also promised that if we believe in him we will never be thirsty again. What kind of thirst do you believe Jesus can quench? How has this been true in your life?

Allow for 10 to 15 minutes of discussion; then gather everyone. Ask people to share more God Sightings arising from their discussions.

Go Forward

Instruct members to pick up their plates and cups and to imagine they're standing in front of Jesus, waiting to be fed. Ask them to silently consider these two questions:

❧How would you describe the current intensity of your hunger and thirst for God?

❧What is the deepest hunger that you need Jesus to satisfy in your life right now?

Ask everyone to pray silently. Close by thanking God for promising to satisfy each and every person's deepest need.

Bonus Idea

Plan to eat together this week. The event can be as simple as a tasty snack or as elaborate as dinner out as a group.

Free to See

Before you gather:

In this get-together, you'll test people's ability to follow directions in a confusing visual test. On a large sheet of white poster board, write "red," "green," and "blue" multiple times, using thick red, blue, and green markers. Be sure the color of the marker does not match the word. For example, use a blue or green marker to write "red," and use a red or green marker to write "blue." Write the words randomly so they are in no discernible order. Write them small enough to fill the poster board with about five lines of text with six or more words to a line. Have a stopwatch or timer available.

Learning to Experience God Every Day

Welcome everyone. Ask each person to tell about a God Sighting that happened this week.

Go!

After everyone has had a chance to share, ask for three volunteers to try a vision test.

Say: **You must read the words as fast as you can. I will be timing you to see who can read the fastest with the least number of mistakes.** Ask the rest of the group to cheer the volunteers on and to try to keep track of their mistakes.

(Hint: This test is difficult because the word tells your brain one thing, but the color of the word tells your brain another, so sometimes people will start "reading" the *color* of the letters instead of the word itself. Performance is not as important as the experience of this test—trying to handle two conflicting signals at once!)

After three people have taken turns completing the test, compare their results and ask:

❧ Week 20—May 14-20

1 Samuel 15–28; John 8:1–11:54;
Psalms 110–117; Proverbs 15:8-23

❧What challenged you in this test, and how did you respond to those challenges?

After the volunteers have had a chance to share, explain that this is a test of "mental flexibility"—of the brain's ability to do one thing while another part of the brain is trying to do something else. Here's what's happening: One part of the brain is trying to translate the *letters* into a word, but another part of the brain is translating the *color* of the letters into a word. So sometimes people get the signals mixed up and call the word *red* "blue" because the word is written in blue!

Go Deeper

Form teams of four or five, and allow everyone a chance to experience the test for themselves. When people aren't taking the test, have them discuss:

❧Describe a time this past week when you felt as if your brain was trying to do two things at once. What emotions did that spark?

❧How was this test similar to what you sometimes experience when you try to focus on God? What distracts you?

Go Forward

After every team has had a chance to try the test and discuss the questions, gather everyone. Ask for a volunteer to repeat the test—with some changes—in front of the group.

Say: **You must read the *colors* instead of the words, but you can take as much time as you want to complete the test.**

Ask the volunteer to share the experience with the group. What was easier about this version of the test? more difficult?

Ask everyone to find a partner to discuss:

❧Imagine the words on the board are the things you know are God's will for your life, and the colors are the things that lure you away from God's will. What can you do to resist the temptations and stay focused on God's will?

Ask a volunteer to read John 8:34-36 out loud. Close in prayer, thanking God for giving you the freedom through Jesus to resist the temptations of the world. Ask God to increase members' mental and spiritual flexibility, so they can stay focused on God in the midst of the distractions and temptations of their lives. Pray for this increased flexibility to allow them to experience more God Sightings in the week ahead.

Apart or Connected?

....

Before you gather:
Provide a glass of water and three drinking straws for each member
of your group. (Optional: Instead of water, provide fruit smoothies
for this experience.)

....

Learning to Experience God Every Day

Welcome everyone. Ask each person to tell about a God Sighting that
happened this week.

Go!

After everyone has had a chance to share, give everyone a glass of
water with two drinking straws on the side. Ask people to follow these
instructions before enjoying their drink:

❧ **You must use both straws. Place one straw inside the glass and
one straw outside the glass. Now place your mouth over the
ends of both straws and drink! Having trouble? Try again!**

Ask people why they think it was hard to drink with two straws. After
a few minutes, allow members to use just one straw to enjoy the water
while you continue your discussion.

Go Deeper

Say: **When you drink through a straw, you begin by lowering the pressure in your mouth. But with one straw outside the glass, you continue to bring air inside your mouth. This keeps the pressure the same inside and outside your mouth, making it hard to drink.**

Form groups of four to discuss:

❧Describe a time during the past week when you tried to connect with God and felt as if you were getting nothing. What emotions did you experience?

Ask a volunteer read John 15:5. Ask:

❧What things in your life resemble the "outside" straw and hinder you in your attempts to connect with God?

❧Share the struggles and victories you've experienced in the past week in your attempts to connect with God. What God Sightings helped you stay connected? Which Scripture readings helped?

Go Forward

Gather the entire group, and share highlights from the small group discussions. Give everyone a new straw, and ask people to imagine that the straws represent their connection to the vine Jesus describes in John 15:5. Encourage them to use the clean straws as Bible bookmarks to remind them of this connection. Discuss:

❧How can you connect with God and drink more deeply from God's Word this week?

Close your time together in prayer, thanking God for what he has shown you about the importance of staying connected to Jesus. Then ask everyone to spend a moment in personal silent prayer, thanking God for the way he connects the members of your group with one another and with him.

Aha Moments

Before you gather:

Make a list of 10 small objects that are difficult to spot in your meeting room. Use creative descriptions or names (such as "yellow stick with a red top" for a pencil) to make the activity more challenging. Photocopy a list for each member, and provide pens or pencils. Arrange the lighting to make it easy to darken the room.

Learning to Experience God Every Day

Welcome everyone. Ask each person to tell about a God Sighting that happened this week.

Go!

After everyone has had a chance to share, give each person a list of objects. Explain that people should look for the items in the room. Tell people they need to work individually; no one should talk to or help another person. People will have two minutes to find the items; touching or moving objects is not allowed.

Start the activity; then after one minute, darken the room. Allow another minute for people to continue their search before turning the lights back on. Ask how many objects people found. Then discuss:

☙**What one word describes how you felt when the lights went out?**

After a few minutes of sharing, tell people they'll now repeat the exercise, but with new rules. This time they may help one another, and anyone who discovers an object will shout, "Aha!" so everyone else knows where to find it. People may also ask for help at any time. The lights will remain on, and people will have two more minutes to complete the activity.

❧**WEEK 22—May 28–June 3**

2 Samuel 13–21; John 17–Acts 1;
Psalms 119:81–121:8; Proverbs 16:6-18

After two minutes, tally the number of items people found this time. Discuss:

❧ **The second time, you were able to share discoveries. How does sharing your God Sightings each week help others see more of God?**

Go Deeper

Form groups of three or four, and discuss:

❧ **Describe an "aha" moment of discovery you had this week during your Bible reading or everyday life. How was this moment a God Sighting?**

❧ **Read Psalm 119:105, and describe how you experience God's Word as a light for your path.**

Go Forward

Gather everyone, and ask each person to complete this sentence:

❧ **"I experienced an aha moment during our time together when…"**

Encourage members to write down the aha moments they experience with God during Scripture reading or in everyday life in the coming week. Have them note the factors that helped them discover an important truth, direction, or understanding. Was it because they persevered through the darkness until the light came on? listened to someone share a God Sighting? allowed God to change their thinking, instead of relying on their own understanding?

Close in prayer, thanking God for the light of his Word and the way he's opening people's eyes and hearts to aha moments—God Sightings—every day.

Standing in Strength

Learning to Experience God Every Day

Welcome everyone. Ask each person to tell about a God Sighting that happened this week.

Go!

After everyone has had a chance to share, have your group form a circle around a comfortable chair with a back. Ask for two volunteers to complete a strength challenge. (Note: People who have experienced pain or other problems with their arms, necks, or shoulders should not volunteer.)

Have one person sit in the chair, lean back, and get as relaxed and comfortable as possible.

Ask the seated person to lift his or her right arm straight out in front so it's horizontal to the floor, with the palm facing down.

Tell the seated person to try to keep his or her arm and body in the same position during the test. Have another volunteer place a hand just above the seated person's elbow and apply slow, downward pressure to the seated person's arm until it moves slightly.

Now have the seated person sit on the *edge* of the chair (without back support), lift the right arm again, brace himself or herself by tightening back and stomach muscles, and then complete the same strength test. Ask the seated person:

❧**Were you stronger or weaker in this position?**

Now ask the seated person to stand with his or her legs about a foot apart, and repeat the challenge. Ask:

❧**WEEK 23—June 4-10**

2 Samuel 22–1 Kings 7; Acts 2:1–7:50;
Psalms 122–128; Proverbs 16:19-33

✎Were you stronger or weaker in this position?

Repeat the strength test with additional volunteers; if time allows, encourage everyone to take part.

Go Deeper

Form groups of three or four, and discuss:

✎How is this strength test an illustration of what could happen if your *faith* were tested?

✎How strong do you think your faith really is? Are you comfortable and somewhat weak, sitting up strong, or standing firm and at your strongest?

Ask a volunteer to read 2 Corinthians 13:4 and Acts 5:38-39.

✎Describe a time you felt weak but experienced God's power to strengthen you to do things you knew you couldn't do alone.

✎How do regular God Sightings prepare you to draw strength from God?

Go Forward

In closing, ask people to stand, pick up their Bibles, and hold them in their right hands with their right arms outstretched. Encourage people to hold their Bibles in this position for 30 seconds as they consider the following two questions:

✎How has the Bible reading you've done over the last 23 weeks strengthened you?

✎How can you tap into God's strength in times of testing in the next week?

Close in prayer, asking God for his strength to stand strong in the face of life's tests.

In Sync or Out of Tune?

Before you gather:
Have a few extra Bibles on hand to make sure everyone has one
during your get-together.

Learning to Experience God Every Day

Welcome everyone. Ask each person to tell about a God Sighting
that happened this week.

Go!

After everyone has had a chance to share, make sure each person
has a Bible. Ask everyone to open the Bible to Psalms 129–135
and to choose one psalm to read aloud so everyone can hear.
When you say "go," instruct each person to start reading out
loud—all at the same time. (Then plug your ears!) Allow the
reading to go on for a minute—or less if the noise is unbearable!

Ask people to describe in one word how they felt during the
activity. Discuss what people didn't like about everyone reading
all at once.

Go Deeper

Form groups of three or four to discuss:

> ◆Share an experience you had this past week that made
> you feel the same emotion you felt during the activity.

◆**WEEK 24—June 11-17**

1 Kings 8:1–18:46; Acts 7:51–11:30;
Psalms 129–135; Proverbs 17:1-13

❧What was happening around you that was similar to what you just experienced?

Say: **Life often feels chaotic, noisy, and out of sync. And it's even worse when we are out of sync with the people around us.**

Ask a volunteer to read Psalm 133:1-3, and ask small groups to discuss:

❧Describe a time in the past week when you experienced harmony and unity. How "precious" are these times to you?

❧How can you *hear* God Sightings in your life?

❧How can you influence the level of harmony in your world?

Go Forward

Gather everyone, and close by sharing a time of fellowship, unity, and harmony. Get a jump-start on the next week's readings by asking people to turn to Psalm 136. Tell them they will repeat the activity they did earlier, only this time everyone will read Psalm 136:1-4 out loud together.

After the unified reading, ask people to think about the harmony God brings to their lives and ways they've seen or heard God in that harmony during the past week. Then challenge each person to think of just one way to make a relationship more harmonious in the upcoming week.

Finally, ask God to refresh you to live in harmony with the people around you in the coming week.

Identity Theft!

....

....

Learning to Experience God Every Day

Welcome everyone. Ask each person to tell about a God Sighting that happened this week.

Go!

After everyone has had a chance to share, ask people to take out the form of identification they brought with them and to look at it to answer the following questions:

❧What information on your ID helps identify you? What one thing on this ID would help protect your identity the most?

Now ask people to put their forms of identification into the box or bag you're holding. Keep the IDs as the group discusses:

❧Describe with one word how you felt when you gave me your ID. Why?

❧What would you do if your ID were stolen? Why is it so valuable to you?

❧WEEK 25—June 18-24

1 Kings 19–2 Kings 7; Acts 12:1–16:15;
Psalms 136–142; Proverbs 17:14-25

Go Deeper

Form groups of three or four to discuss:

❧ **Your ID describes you, but what words would you use to describe yourself? If you're honest, do you most often think of yourself in a positive or negative way?**

Ask a volunteer to read Psalm 139:13-14; then ask:

❧ **When you see yourself in the mirror, do you see God's workmanship? Why or why not?**

❧ **What changes do you need to make to see more of God in yourself? in others?**

❧ **Most of us protect ourselves from identity theft, but what about the thief who can steal our identity in Christ? How does Satan try to steal your identity?**

Go Forward

Bring the entire group together, and return everyone's ID. Have people place their IDs in the palm of one hand and hold it outstretched during your prayer time. Ask people to close their eyes as you read the words of Psalm 139:13-16. Then pray, asking God for his protection from the thief who tries to steal our identity in Christ. Pray for God to help people glimpse God as they consider how wonderfully they are made during the coming week.

Three Steps to Better Vision

Before you gather:
Plan for a portion (or all, if weather and space permit) of this meeting to be held outdoors. Be sure to have chairs or blankets for everyone to sit on.

Learning to Experience God Every Day

Welcome everyone. Ask each person to tell about a God Sighting that happened this week.

Go!

Congratulations to you and your small group for all you've seen and shared so far on your God Sightings journey. Because of your perseverance, your ability to see God's presence in your life in new and exciting ways has most certainly improved. Now it's time for a checkup so that as you begin the next phase, you'll recognize God in your life more than ever. So gather your fellow God-watchers, head outside, and try this!

Ask people to locate an object in their surroundings that's just beyond their clear field of vision—one that's slightly blurry. Next instruct them to:

1. Touch their index fingers and thumbs of the opposite hands together to form an O shape.

2. Collapse the O so that their fingers and thumbs are in a pinch position, but still in contact with the opposite finger and thumb. (They should see a small hole in the middle where their fingers and thumbs meet.)

3. Find the blurry object and with one eye look through the small hole at it. What happens?

Ask people to continue to test their "personal magnifiers" for the next five minutes with other items, including words, fabric, or even the features of someone's face.

Say: **Pair up and share how a personal magnifier like this could help you see God more clearly.**

Go Deeper

Form groups of three or four, and ask a volunteer to read Psalm 144:3. Discuss:

❧**Do you regularly feel noticed by God? Why or why not?**

❧**Think about all you've discovered over the past six months as you've been on the lookout for God. How do you see things differently now? How have your habits changed? your attitudes?**

Have people repeat the steps to make a personal magnifier with their fingers and scan the environment again. Instruct them to stop when they notice something they didn't see before and share with their group:

❧**What new thing did you see? Why do you think you missed it before? How did the magnifier help you see it?**

❧**How can you make a magnifier in your heart to help you see God more frequently and more clearly?**

Go Forward

Gather everyone, and ask people to share the highlights of the God Sightings they experienced during their time together. Wrap up the discussion by asking:

❧**God is able to see us in the midst of everything, but it's often difficult for us to see God in the busy-ness and complexity of the world we live in. What are three steps you could take to help you recognize God's presence in your life?**

Close in prayer, thanking God for his presence in your lives and for all the God Sightings your group has experienced. Ask God to help you see him with greater clarity in the weeks ahead.

God's Advice Column

Before you gather:
Clip an advice column from the newspaper, or do an Internet search for "Dear Abby" and print a recent bit of advice.

Learning to Experience God Every Day

Welcome everyone. Ask each person to tell about a God Sighting that happened this week.

Go!

After everyone has had a chance to share, read the advice-column question you chose from the newspaper or Internet. Ask people how they think the adviser will respond to the dilemma.

Go Deeper

Have a volunteer read Psalm 1:1-2. Have everyone find a partner and discuss:

❧Tell about a time you followed advice that was not biblical. What were the results? What about a time you followed God's advice, even though it didn't make sense in the eyes of the world? What were the results?

❧**WEEK 27—July 2-8**

2 Kings 20–1 Chronicles 6; Acts 21:18–26:32; Psalms 150; 1–6; Proverbs 18:9-21

Go Forward

Call the group together. Reread the question from the advice column, as well as the answer. Congratulate those who came close to guessing the "right" answer. Ask:

❧**If you based your answer on what you think Jesus would do, how would you respond to the person seeking advice?**

Encourage people to share specific advice they would give, based on what the Bible teaches rather than on how they feel.

Have people return to their partners and discuss:

❧**What's one new thing God has shown you through this week's reading? Is God prompting you to do something that might not make sense in the eyes of the world?**

Ask partners to spend a few minutes praying for each other and the decisions they're facing. Encourage them not to offer advice, but to simply pray for the other person.

A Lesson From Nature

Before you gather:
You'll need a small piece of ice for each person and hand towels.

Learning to Experience God Every Day

Welcome everyone. Ask each person to tell about a God Sighting that happened this week.

Go!

After everyone has had a chance to share, ask people to close their eyes and visualize the worst storm they've ever experienced. Prompt them to remember what they saw, tasted, smelled, heard, and touched and how all of it made them feel. After about a minute, ask people to open their eyes. Ask for volunteers to tell about the storm they were remembering and how it affected them and others who experienced it.

Have everyone find a partner and discuss:

❧**What did the storm tell you about God?**

After five minutes, pull the group together, and debrief insights from the pairs' discussions.

❧**WEEK 28—July 9-15**

1 Chronicles 7–21; Acts 27:1–Romans 3:8;
Psalms 7–11; Proverbs 18:22–19:12

Go Deeper

Have a volunteer read Romans 1:20. As a group discuss:

❧**According to this verse, there is no excuse for not knowing God. What can you say you know—really know— about God simply by looking at his creation? Why? How has this knowledge affected the way you go about life?**

Go Forward

Have people return to their partners and discuss:

❧**What storm in your life are you facing this week? How, specifically, do you think God's "eternal power and divine nature" can help?**

After allowing some time for discussion, ask everyone to come together as a group. Give everyone a small ice chip to hold. Ask people to close their eyes and recall an ice storm, a blizzard, or a time they experienced the cold.

Say: **As this ice melts in the warmth of your hands, visualize God's power in the midst of life's storms.**

Allow a minute or so for the ice chips to melt. As you pass towels around for people to use to dry their hands, ask:

❧**How was this experience like the storms you've experienced in your life?**

After everyone has had a chance to share, take a moment for silent prayer. Encourage people to ask God to calm the storms they face in their lives right now.

Close by thanking God for all of the traits of God that people mentioned during their discussions.

The Gift of God

Before you gather:
Collect enough small stones so each person will have one. Select stones with a relatively flat surface. You'll also need fine-tipped markers.

Learning to Experience God Every Day

Welcome everyone. Ask each person to tell about a God Sighting that happened this week.

Go!

After everyone has had a chance to share, give everyone a small stone. Have each person find a partner, hold a stone, and discuss:

> ❧ **Think of a time you were dealing with a specific sin and needed forgiveness. What was the effect of that sin in your life? How did it influence your relationship with God? with others?**

After five minutes, ask pairs to share insights with the entire group.

❧ **WEEK 29—July 16-22**

1 Chronicles 22:1–2 Chronicles 8:10; Romans 3:9–8:8; Psalms 12:1–18:15; Proverbs 19:13-25

Go Deeper

Ask a volunteer to read Romans 6:22-23. Discuss:

✎ **If you've ever been able to release a sin to God, what happened? How did it change your view of yourself? of God?**

Go Forward

Ask people to look at their stones and consider these questions:

✎ **In what area of your life do you still need assurance that God can bring about change? Do you believe God *can* bring about change?**

Give everyone a marker. Ask people to think of a few words or symbols that remind them of their sin and then write the words or symbols on the stones.

Have people place the stones in their shoes and take a short walk outside. As a group, discuss:

✎ **How is walking with a stone in your shoe like carrying the sin your stone represents?**

✎ **If you really believed what God says in Romans 6:22-23, what would you be doing differently?**

Depending on where you're meeting, have members throw their stones in either a trash can or an open field or lake. Gather to thank God for freeing us from the bondage of sin and for his gift of eternal life.

Living Sacrifices

Before you gather:

Cut curling ribbon into 8-inch strips; you'll need one strip for each person. Also have scissors or butter knives on hand.

Learning to Experience God Every Day

Welcome everyone. Ask each person to tell about a God Sighting that happened this week.

Go!

After everyone has had a chance to share, distribute strips of curling ribbon. Discuss:

❧ **Think of a time you offered someone a particular gift that gave you great satisfaction. How was the gift received? Why did it give you joy to offer the gift?**

Go Deeper

Read Romans 12:1. Form pairs to discuss:

❧ **How is your life a gift to God? What about your life do you think is especially pleasing to God? What may need to change to make your life a more pleasing gift?**

❧ **WEEK 30—July 23-29**

2 Chronicles 8:11–25:28; Romans 8:9–12:21;
Psalms 18:16–22:31; Proverbs 19:26–20:10

Go Forward

Have everyone remain in pairs and discuss:

➤ Ribbon can be shaped in a lot of ways, for many different uses. How is God reshaping your life through your
Bible reading? through the people and events in your life?
through this small group experience?

➤ What would your life look like if you consciously made it
a living sacrifice? Are you willing to give yourself as this
kind of gift to God?

Bring people together. Provide scissors or butter knives, and
have people curl their ribbons by quickly pulling them over the
scissors' or knives' edges. Ask people how their lives are being
transformed by the God Sightings they're experiencing.

Spend time in prayer, thanking God for the renewal he brings to
each life. Encourage group members to take their ribbons home
and use them as Bible bookmarks to remind them to live each
day as people transformed by God's love.

Perfect Save

Before you gather:
Have a newspaper on hand. You'll also need paper and a pen for everyone.

Learning to Experience God Every Day

Welcome everyone; then give each person a section of the newspaper, and have people scan their sections for the best news they can find. Take a few minutes to discuss and laugh over some of the stories they find. Ask everyone:

❧**How did you see God at work this week? How did he show up in your life or the life of someone you know or have read about? Tell us the best news of your week— your God Sightings!**

Go!

After everyone has had a chance to share, ask a volunteer to read 1 Corinthians 1:18. As a group, discuss:

❧**Have you ever shared the best news of all—Jesus—with someone who wasn't ready to hear about him? Tell about the experience and how you felt.**

❧**WEEK 31—July 30–August 5**

2 Chronicles 26–Ezra 2; Romans 13:1–1 Corinthians 2:5; Psalms 23–27; Proverbs 20:11-23

Go Deeper

Form pairs to discuss:

>In what ways have you seen, firsthand, the power of the Cross? In the changed life of a friend? In your own changed life? How does what you've seen encourage you to continue sharing your faith?

>Is God prompting you to talk to someone about him? What do you think God is nudging you to do? What's stopping you?

Go Forward

Gather everyone to discuss:

>The word *gospel* means good news, and it truly is the best news humanity has ever received. But to many people, it doesn't seem like news at all. How are your God Sightings starting to change that perception within your circle of family and friends?

Encourage pairs to pray for each other and the people God is prompting them to tell about him. Thank God that he doesn't leave us as he finds us, but through his power, changes us and gives us hope.

Shelter From the Storm

....

Before you gather:
Gather a blanket and/or pillow for each person in your group.

....

Learning to Experience God Every Day

Welcome everyone. Ask each person to tell about a God Sighting that happened this week.

Go!

After everyone has had a chance to share, give everyone a blanket and/or pillow. Encourage people to use the blankets and pillows to get really comfortable.

Ask people to close their eyes and think about these questions:

❧**Think about a time you felt completely safe. Where were you? Who, if anyone, was with you? What was the lighting like? Do you remember any scents? any sounds?**

After a few minutes of silent reflection, ask people to open their eyes. Encourage volunteers to share their memories of feeling safe. Say: **Some people may always have felt safe. Some may have felt safe as children but don't now. Others may have felt safe with a spouse who is now gone. Some people—maybe even some of us—have never felt truly safe. Some of us may actually live in fear.**

❧**WEEK 32—August 6-12**

Ezra 3:1–Nehemiah 5:13; 1 Corinthians
2:6–7:40; Psalms 28–32; Proverbs 20:24–21:7

Go Deeper

Ask for a volunteer to read Psalm 32:7. Ask everyone to find a partner and discuss:

❧ **It takes trust to depend upon something or someone to protect you. What reasons did you find this week to trust God?**

❧ **When has God's protection been especially evident in your life?**

Go Forward

Ask people to snuggle up in their blankets or rest on their pillows and discuss with a partner:

❧ **What are the benefits of resting in God's protection?**

❧ **What would it look like for God to be your hiding place or protection this week? What's keeping you from allowing him to be that for you?**

Spend a few moments thanking God for his protection and for being a place of refuge. As a group, pray that God will draw each of you close and replace fear with peace and confidence.

The Way Out...and Onward

Before you gather:
Have paper and pens on hand.

Learning to Experience God Every Day

After you've welcomed everyone, ask each person to tell about a God Sighting that happened this week.

Go!

After everyone has had a chance to share, ask the group to form a circle. Ask people to place in the middle of the circle any items in the room or items they brought with them that could represent temptation. (Be sure to choose one yourself!) People might choose an unhealthy snack, a DVD, a wallet, or a laptop, for example. If possible, form same-sex pairs and discuss:

❧ **Why do you think you're especially vulnerable to this type of temptation?**

Go Deeper

Gather the group, and ask a volunteer to read 1 Corinthians 10:13. Discuss:

❧This verse says God is faithful, meaning God does what he says he'll do. How does knowing this encourage you when you're facing temptation?

❧How have you seen God during times of temptation?

Go Forward

Give everyone a sheet of paper and a pen. Say: **First Corinthians 10:13 says God will provide a way out when we're tempted. Look around the room, and identify objects that can help you escape temptation.** People might identify a trash can, a phone, a family picture, tennis shoes, or some kind of athletic equipment, for example. Have each person think of a specific temptation and then list ways God might provide a way out.

Ask people to return to their partners and tell about what they wrote, divulging as much as they're comfortable sharing. Discuss:

❧What will you do the next time you're tempted to do something you know is not pleasing to God? Share the specific action you'll take.

Ask pairs to pray for each other now and during the week, and encourage them to take their papers home and put them where they're most likely to face temptation—on the refrigerator, by the computer, or in the car, for example. Remind them that whenever they resist temptation, they've experienced a God Sighting!

Swallowed

....

Before you gather:
Pour a glass of water for each person.

....

Learning to Experience God Every Day

Welcome everyone. Ask each person to tell about a God Sighting that happened this week.

Go!

After everyone has had a chance to share, say: **Now we're going to discuss something that none of us likes to talk about— death. Death is a big deal. Like other hard things, it's scary and out of our control. But just like all the other hard things in our lives, it's *not* bigger than God. Jesus swallowed it up!**

Ask everyone to take a glass of water and drink it down—the whole glass. (Have people keep the glasses for later.)

Ask a volunteer to read aloud 1 Corinthians 15:54b-57; then form pairs to discuss:

❧We know that we will all experience a physical death. So what does the Bible mean when it says death is "swallowed up in victory"?

❧What does it mean to you to know that, just as you swallowed the water and now it's gone, Christ has swallowed death for you?

❧WEEK 34—August 20-26

Esther 8–Job 22; 1 Corinthians 12:27–2 Corinthians 1:11; Psalms 37–40; Proverbs 21:23–22:4

Go Deeper

Gather the group and say:

Look at your empty glass. Picture it being filled with all the hard things you face in life: difficult relationships, habits you can't break, circumstances you never wanted or asked for, and even death. Now remember that Christ has already drunk this glass for you. He has achieved victory over death; he can give you victory over the sins that still plague you and comfort you in the midst of your struggles.

Have people close their eyes and picture Christ drinking the water that was in their glasses, swallowing all that sin and death. Encourage everyone to spend a few minutes in silent prayer, thanking God for what he has done and for what it means to each person in the group.

Go Forward

Have everyone find a partner and discuss:

When have you seen God victorious—either in your life or in the life of someone you know?

Pray together, thanking Christ for his sacrifice for you and his victory in your life. Place your struggles in his hands, and ask him to remind you daily that he is with you in the midst of every struggle.

Not From Ourselves

Before you gather:

Provide a variety of drinking vessels, such as a cracked bowl, a crystal wine goblet, or a brightly painted mug. (Optional: Invite people to each bring a cup or bowl that they think somehow represents them.)

Learning to Experience God Every Day

Welcome everyone. Ask each person to tell about a God Sighting that happened this week.

Go!

After everyone has shared, have people select a bowl or cup that they think represents them. Ask them to explain their choices. Then have someone read 2 Corinthians 4:7 aloud. Discuss:

❧**God made each of our vessels different, but ultimately, we're just vessels. How does this verse affect the way you view yourself? God?**

❧**WEEK 35—August 27–September 2**

Job 23–42; Ecclesiastes 1–3; 2 Corinthians 1:12–6:13; Psalms 41–46; Proverbs 22:5-15

Go Deeper

Form pairs to discuss:

❧ **This verse makes it clear that our power comes from God—not our own abilities. How have you experienced the power of God this week? through the time you've spent with him? in a difficult situation?**

Go Forward

Bring the group together, and have people hold the vessels they chose. Say: **Think about how you, like your bowl or cup, are ultimately weak and finite. Then think about God—his power and light and strength. Picture this light inside you, inside your cup or bowl, and picture the strength it gives you.**

Allow a few moments for reflection, and then have everyone find a partner and discuss:

❧ **What specific action step do you think God might want you to take in response to what he has shown you this week?**

Spend some time praying as a group. Thank God for his infinite power. Thank him for choosing to fill each of you with his light. Ask him to help you apply what he has shown you to your lives.

Remember

Before you gather:
Cut a length of string for each person. The strings should be long enough to tie on a finger.

Learning to Experience God Every Day

Welcome everyone. Ask each person to tell about a God Sighting that happened this week.

Go!

After people have had a chance to share, ask them to briefly brainstorm techniques they've used to remind themselves of something (such as a note on the hand, a rubber band on the wrist, or something set in a visible place).

Read Ecclesiastes 12:1 aloud together. Give each person a length of string, and tell people to help each other tie the strings on their fingers to help them remember their Creator. As a group discuss:

❧How often during your average day do you remember God?

❧Are there particular ways God tries to get your attention throughout your day? What does this look like?

❧**WEEK 36—September 3-9**

Ecclesiastes 4–Isaiah 5; 2 Corinthians
6:14–11:15; Psalms 47–53; Proverbs 22:16-29

Go Deeper

Form pairs to discuss:

❧ **Why does it matter whether or not we remember God?**

❧ **What attribute of God has been important for you to remember this week? Explain your answer.**

Go Forward

Gather the group, and discuss these questions:

❧ **Is there one thing you feel compelled to do or change in your life in response to what you read this week?**

❧ **Is there some practical way, like tying a string around your finger, you can remind yourself each day of God and of the step he is guiding you to take next?**

Have everyone hold up the finger with the string tied to it. Emphasize that it's pointing up, toward God, which is the same attitude our hearts and minds should take. As you keep your fingers pointing up, pray together. Ask God to make you aware of the ways he's reminding you of him, and thank him for caring enough to reach out to get your attention.

Wonderful, Mighty, Everlasting...

Before you gather:
You'll need markers, tape, and two sheets of 8½ x 11-inch paper per person.

Learning to Experience God Every Day

Welcome everyone. Ask each person to tell about a God Sighting that happened this week.

Go!

After everyone has had a chance to share, distribute paper and markers. Have someone read Isaiah 9:6 aloud.

Say: **"Wonderful Counselor, Mighty God, Everlasting Father, Prince of Peace." God is known by many different names, and there is much we can learn about his character as we think about the names for God that we find in his Word.**

Have people think about what they've read in the past weeks and reflect on what they've learned about who God is. Give everyone a few minutes to reflect on these questions:

❧If you could choose one adjective, like *wonderful, mighty,* or *everlasting,* to describe one of the most important things you've learned about God recently, what would it be?

- If you could choose one noun or role, like *prince* or *counselor,* to describe one of the most important things you've learned about God recently, what would it be?

Have people write the adjectives and nouns they came up with—one on each sheet of paper. Then tape the papers to the wall. Ask people to explain why they chose those particular words.

Go Deeper

Form pairs and discuss:

- Think of a difficult situation you faced this week. How would it have changed you or the situation if you had seen God as a wonderful counselor? a loving Father? a mighty warrior?

- Look at the words on the wall. In what ways does knowing God's name make responding to him easier? harder?

Go Forward

Gather the group and discuss:

- Think of the two words you wrote. How has God shown up in your life in a way that defines these two words?

- Is there one thing you feel God is calling you to do in response to what you discovered about him this week?

Have each person say a one-sentence prayer to thank God for who he is and how he reveals himself through his names.

Before they leave, remind people to remove their papers from the wall, take them home, and put them in a prominent place as reminders that God remains the same and is who he says he is.

God's Fruit Salad

Before you gather:

Purchase different varieties of fruit, such as apples, bananas, oranges, pears, pineapples, kiwis, mangoes, and star fruit. You'll also need a large bowl, a knife for each person, and bowls and forks or spoons.

Learning to Experience God Every Day

Welcome everyone. Ask each person to tell about a God Sighting that happened this week.

Go!

After everyone has had a chance to share, gather the group in the kitchen. Spend some time together cutting up the fruit and placing it in a large bowl to make a fruit salad. Be sure everyone is involved. As you work, discuss the unique attributes of each kind of fruit.

Ask a volunteer to read Galatians 5:22-23. As a group discuss:

❧Why do you think these attributes are called *fruit* of the Spirit?

❧Tell about someone who exhibits a fruit of the Spirit. How have you seen it affect the lives of others?

❧**WEEK 38—September 17-23**

Isaiah 25:1–43:13; Galatians 3:10–Ephesians 2:22; Psalms 61–67; Proverbs 23:17–35

Go Deeper

Form pairs and discuss:

❧ To produce the best fruit, a tree must be pruned. How have you felt God "pruning" you during the past week?

❧ Which fruit would you most like to develop in your life? Why that particular one?

Go Forward

As a group, discuss:

❧ Love. Joy. Peace. Patience. Kindness. Goodness. Faithfulness. Gentleness. Self-control. In what situations have you seen any of these traits displayed this week? Tell us about more God Sightings!

As you're wrapping up, serve the fruit salad, and encourage everyone to enjoy the sweet and various flavors. Point out that the flavors blend together, even though each one tastes so different. Just like the fruit of the Spirit!

While you eat, ask people to tell the group about a fruit of the Spirit they see in the life of another group member.

Every Part's Important

....

Before you gather:

Set out a few board games. Remove a part of each game, such as the dice, a timer, some of the playing pieces, or other small but essential parts. You'll also need paper, pen, and an envelope for each person.

....

Learning to Experience God Every Day

Welcome everyone. Ask each person to tell about a God Sighting that happened this week.

Go!

After everyone has had a chance to share, ask people to play board games for about five minutes. See what happens when they discover parts are missing. Briefly discuss the experience of playing a game without all the parts.

Go Deeper

Ask a volunteer to read Ephesians 4:15-16. As a group discuss:

❧**What would our group be like if some of us were missing? What would our church be like if some of the people in it were missing?** Be sure the group discusses people who work behind the scenes.

❧**WEEK 39—September 24-30**

Isaiah 43:14–62:5; Ephesians 3:1–Philippians 2:18; Psalms 68–72; Proverbs 24:1-12

Say: **Each part of the church body—even the small, seemingly unimportant parts—is essential for the body as a whole to function.** Form pairs to discuss:

❧What is your role in the Christian body? Give examples of how God is using you, even if you consider the examples unimportant. If you don't have a role, why don't you? What gifts or talents do you have that could strengthen and encourage the church?

❧In the past few weeks, when have you seen God at church? Was it in the warm hug of a greeter or the small band of brothers who repainted the nursery? Maybe it was in the high school kids who went on a missions trip?

Go Forward

Gather everyone and discuss:

❧Why do you think God gave us each certain gifts and talents to use, instead of making everyone good at everything?

Give each person paper, a pen, and an envelope. Ask people to each write a note to someone they've seen God using to build up the body of Christ. They might choose the pastor or the custodian, the secretary or the volunteer who cleans nursery toys—anyone who has allowed them to glimpse God at work. Ask people to label the envelopes, and then collect the envelopes to distribute tomorrow.

As a group, pray that each person would know how important he or she is to the body of Christ. Ask God to help your group be an encouragement to others who are discouraged in their roles or unsure of their value to the body of Christ.

Don't Stop Running

Before you gather:
Download a clip from the movie *Facing the Giants* by searching for
"*Facing the Giants* death crawl" on YouTube.

Learning to Experience God Every Day

Welcome everyone. Ask each person to tell about a God Sighting
that happened this week.

Go!

After everyone has had a chance to share, show the YouTube clip
from *Facing the Giants*. Discuss:

❧There are times when being a Christian is hard, when the
choices you make go against the culture or the understanding of others. Tell about a situation you've faced in which
giving in to social pressures or the beliefs of others would
have been the easy thing to do. What did you do?

❧Brock reached a point where he felt he couldn't go any
farther, when the pain threatened to overwhelm him. How
do you keep pressing on when things get difficult?

❧ **WEEK 40—October 1-7**
Isaiah 62:6–Jeremiah 9:26; Philippians 2:19–
Colossians 3:17; Psalms 73:1–78:55; Proverbs 24:13-27

Go Deeper

Read Philippians 3:13-14. Form pairs and discuss:

❧ **When have you seen God show up in the midst of a situation that seemed impossible for you or someone else to face?**

❧ **How have you seen God encourage you to keep going during times of discouragement?**

Go Forward

Say: **Sometimes we're asked to do things that seem impossible to us—the way doing the death crawl across the football field seemed to Brock. We hit a point where we feel that we can't make any more progress, and we want to give up. But God calls us to "press on" toward the goal and continue our work until it's finished.**

In pairs, discuss:

❧ **How did God show up in your life this week in a moment of discouragement or exhaustion? Did you recognize God in that situation? How did you respond?**

❧ **What is the prize God has promised as a reward for finishing the race you're running? How does that encourage you to press on?**

Gather the group, and ask people to close their eyes for a few minutes as they picture themselves running a long race.
Say: **Feel the burn in your muscles and the heaviness in your chest. Everything inside you wants to quit. But up ahead you see Christ and the prize he has waiting for you. Your step quickens, and your determination intensifies. As you focus on Christ, silently ask God to give you the strength to continue on to his finish line, and thank him for the ways he has encouraged you to press on to the end.**

Who Are You Working For?

Before you gather:
You'll need paper and a pen for each person.

Learning to Experience God Every Day

Welcome everyone. Ask each person to tell about a God Sighting that happened this week.

Go!

After everyone has had a chance to share, give each person a piece of paper and a pen. Have people fold the paper into thirds. Tell them that on "go," they'll have 20 seconds to write on one third of the paper as many grocery list–type items as they can.

After 20 seconds have elapsed, ask everyone to imagine that the second third of the paper is an envelope and address it to the president of the United States. Tell people there's no time limit.

Ask them to write a one-sentence valentine to a spouse, child, or someone else they love on the final third, again with no time limit.

When everyone has finished, ask people to look at their papers.

❧How is your handwriting different for each of these exercises? Why do you think it changed, even slightly?

❧How does the quality of your work vary according to who you're doing it for or who will see it?

❧**Week 41—October 8-14**

Jeremiah 10–25; Colossians 3:18–2 Thessalonians 2:17; Psalms 78:56–84:12; Proverbs 24:28–25:15

Go Deeper

Ask a volunteer to read Colossians 3:23-24. Form pairs and discuss:

❧ Whether you work for an international company, a small local business, or your family, what's your attitude as you go about your work? Do you think God is pleased with that attitude? Would you be proud or ashamed for him to see how you go about your days?

❧ How have you seen God active this week in the workplace—in ethics, attitudes, and quality of work?

Go Forward

Gather as a group and discuss:

❧ Tell about someone you saw "working for the Lord" this week. How did he or she affect you and others?

❧ Sometimes our work is as much about our relationships as it is about our vocations. How would working as if the Lord were your master in all things affect your relationships?

As a group, pray that God will help you all realize that everything you do, you ultimately do for him. Ask him to help each of you represent him well in the efforts you put forth.

Written on Your Heart

Learning to Experience God Every Day

Welcome everyone. Ask each person to tell about a God Sighting that happened this week.

Go!

After everyone has had a chance to share, discuss:

➷If you were to get a permanent tattoo, what would it be, why would you choose that particular symbol, and where would you put it?

➷If you have a real tattoo, why was it important for you to have something written permanently on your skin?

Go Deeper

Read Jeremiah 31:33.

Say: **In a sense, you have a soul tattoo. God's commitment to you is written, or etched, on your heart. It can't wear off or be washed away.**

➷**WEEK 42—October 15-21**

Jeremiah 26–38; 2 Thessalonians 3–
1 Timothy 6; Psalms 85–89; Proverbs 25:16-28

Form pairs and discuss:

- What does the permanence of God's love and commitment mean to you?

- When in your life have you seen God's commitment to you expressed most forcibly? How have you expressed your commitment to God?

Go Forward

Gather the group, and debrief some of the insights pairs discovered during their discussions. Then discuss:

- What did God convey to you this week about his commitment to you? Who or what did he place in your life to remind you of his love and commitment?

- How has your connection with God this past week affected how you will live in the coming week?

Close in prayer, thanking God for removing the sins from our hearts and replacing them with his love, permanently written there.

Sweet Instructions

....

Before you gather:
You'll need an old Bible that you don't mind tearing pages out of.

....

Learning to Experience God Every Day

Welcome everyone. Ask each person to tell about a God Sighting that happened this week.

Go!

After everyone has had a chance to share, open the old Bible you brought for this purpose, and say: **You know, I was reading Jeremiah this week, and it didn't make any sense to me. I don't see how it applies to my life, so I think I'm just going to get rid of it.** Proceed to rip out a few pages.

Turn to 2 Timothy, and say: **I also read 2 Timothy, and I didn't like what it says about being gentle toward everyone. I mean, some people don't deserve a gentle response. So I'm going to rip that out, too.**

Rip 2 Timothy out. Then look through the ripped out pages, and read 2 Timothy 3:16-17. Then ask the group:

❧This verse says *all Scripture* is from God and is useful for our lives. **What sections of the Bible do you tend to overlook or ignore? Why?**

❧**How has your daily reading changed your opinion of portions of the Bible that are hard to read?**

❧**WEEK 43—October 22-28**

Jeremiah 39–52; 2 Timothy 1–Titus 3;
Psalms 90–100; Proverbs 26:1-19

Go Deeper

Form pairs and discuss:

- How has your knowledge of God and the Bible helped you in the past week? What situation did you face this week in which more knowledge of the Bible could have helped you?

- Share a passage of Scripture that you've seen come to life, either in your life or in the life of someone you know. What happened?

Go Forward

Bring the group together, and say: **The Bible is our ultimate guide. It prepares us for everything that is happening or will happen. It gives us what we need to deal with every situation. And it gives us guidance to know what's right and what's wrong.**

Have people return to their partners to discuss:

- If you followed God's guide for living all the time, with all your heart, what would you be doing differently right now?

- What changes have you seen in your life since you committed to reading the Bible regularly?

Give each person one page that you tore from the Bible earlier. Ask everyone to jot this note and complete this prayer at the top of the page: "The Bible is my ultimate guide. God, help me _____." Close by asking God to reveal himself clearly to each person this week. Ask God to help you all rely on his guidance through every circumstance in your lives.

A Taste of God

Before you gather:
Ideally you'll have a bruised apple and a sharp paring knife for
each person, including yourself. (You may need to drop several
apples on the floor the day before your meeting, if you don't have
any that are bruised.) If that's not possible, simply have a piece of
fruit and a paring knife on hand for everyone. You'll also need a
bruise-free apple and a felt-tip pen for each person.

Learning to Experience God Every Day

Welcome everyone. Ask each person to tell about a God Sighting
that happened this week.

Go!

After everyone has had a chance to share, ask a volunteer to read
Hebrews 4:12. Explain that a double-edged sword (the term used
in the New International Version) is one that can cut both ways.
It represents being able to remove the bad while promoting the
good—like a surgeon's scalpel, which cuts out just the tumor so
the body can be whole and healthy.

Take a bruised apple and show everyone the bruised spot. Use
a paring knife to cut out the bruise, exposing the healthy flesh
below. (If using a banana, cut out a brown spot. A bruise-free
apple? Cut out the stem. A nectarine? Cut out the pit). Ask:

How is my cutting out the bad part like the way God uses the Bible in our lives?

What did God show you this week through your reading?

Go Deeper

Form pairs and discuss:

Tell about a time God spoke specifically to you through his Word. How did it change you? your thoughts or feelings toward God?

How has God used the Bible this week to cut through your preconceived ideas about him and show you something new?

Go Forward

Gather the group and discuss:

Share a verse from the Bible that has encouraged you. Explain its importance to you.

Give everyone a piece of fruit, a sharp knife, and a pen. Tell people to think of a sin they've been forgiven of, but still feel guilty about. Have them write the sin on the fruit. Then encourage everyone to use a paring knife to cut out the area where the sin is written and throw it away.

Ask pairs to touch base during the week and share how they're continuing to discover God in their readings and in their lives.

Close by enjoying the sweet fruit and thanking God for the gift of his Word and its ability to cut out our sin and leave us spiritually healthy and free.

Pass out bruise-free apples, and encourage people to enjoy them the following day as they read their Bibles.

God's Road Trip

Before you gather:

Prepare or buy brownies or another treat; then set up a treasure hunt. Make three or four clues that will ultimately lead to the hidden snack, or use "Treasure Hunt Clues" at the end of this guide. (The first leads to a clue above a doorway; the second to the windshield of a car; the third under the seat of a chair.) You'll also need paper and a pen for each person.

Learning to Experience God Every Day

Welcome everyone. Ask each person to tell about a God Sighting that happened this week.

Go!

After everyone has had a chance to share, tell people they'll be going on a quick treasure hunt. Give them the first clue, and allow them to work their way to the "treasure." While they're enjoying the snack, discuss:

༄**When you heard we were going on a treasure hunt, what was your first reaction? Maybe you thought the activity is juvenile. Or maybe you expected it to be fun. Or did you think, I'll go along with it, but I'll let the others do the work? Be honest.**

༄**How do our attitudes affect our experiences?**

༄**WEEK 45—November 5-11**

Ezekiel 12–23; Hebrews 7–10; Psalms
105:37–109:31; Proverbs 27:3-13

Go Deeper

Form pairs and discuss:

❧When your attitude has changed toward something or someone, how has the changed attitude affected you, the outcome, or the people around you? Give a specific example.

❧How did God change your attitude toward something this week?

Go Forward

Gather everyone, and share what individuals discovered. Read Ezekiel 18:31. As a group discuss:

❧In what ways do you rebel against God?

❧This verse says to find, or get, a new heart and a new spirit. How can you do that?

Give each person paper and a pen. Have people think of a time God changed their attitude through various events and then draw treasure maps showing how those events led to the changed attitude. Encourage volunteers to share what they've drawn.

Then as a group, pray together. Thank God for always leading us in the right direction. Ask God to help each person be willing to heed his guidance and turn away from things that don't please God.

Encourage group members to use their maps as reminders to continue to seek God every day.

Faith Is...

Before you gather:
You'll need paper and a pen for each person.

Learning to Experience God Every Day

Welcome everyone. Ask each person to tell about a God Sighting that happened this week.

Go!

After everyone has had a chance to share, explain that this week the group will be exploring faith—what it is and where it's seen. Begin by asking people to think of things they know are real but are unable to see or understand—such as time, hunger, gravity, hope, and love. Using hunger as an example, ask:

❧**How do you know hunger is real? You can't see it or touch it. How are you certain it exists?**

Go Deeper

Ask a volunteer to read Hebrews 11:1. Then form pairs, and have partners discuss:

❧**WEEK 46—November 12-18**

Ezekiel 24–38; Hebrews 11:1–James 2:17;
Psalms 110–117; Proverbs 27:14–28:1

✎Faith is being certain of what we can't see. What evidence do you have that Jesus is real? How does he show up in your life, even though you can't see him? in the lives of your family or friends?

✎Tell about a time you questioned your faith or felt it was too small. What happened?

Go Forward

Gather the group to discuss:

✎Not seeing God can sometimes make developing a relationship with him difficult. What is God doing in your life to help you overcome that?

Give everyone a sheet of paper, and ask people to fold the papers in accordion-like pleats. Ask them to write the words of Hebrews 11:1 on an outer edge and then fold up about an inch at the bottom to make a fan. Ask people to use the fans to create a breeze on their face.

Say: **Faith in God is like this breeze on your face. You can't see it, but you know it's there; you can feel it. When you're hot, this small, cool breeze can make a big difference. Our faith in Christ, our confidence in what we cannot see, makes a difference every day, in every situation.**

Pray together, asking God to continue making his presence known and thanking him for the ways he already has made himself known to you.

Lord of My Life

....

Before you gather:
Have on hand worship music and a way to play it. You'll also need paper and a pen for each person.

....

Learning to Experience God Every Day

Have worship music playing as people arrive, and encourage everyone to spend some time praying and worshipping God.

After a few minutes, ask each person to tell about a God Sighting that happened this week.

Go!

After everyone has had a chance to share, ask a volunteer to read 1 Peter 3:15. Discuss:

☙ **What does your worship look like? Are you more likely to enter into a time of worship at church or elsewhere? What prompts you to worship?**

☙ **What do you think it means to worship Christ with every aspect of your life?**

☙ **WEEK 47—November 19-25**
Ezekiel 39:1–Daniel 2:23; James 2:18–1 Peter 4:6; Psalms 118–119:80; Proverbs 28:2-14

Go Deeper

Form pairs to discuss:

❧ What impact would *living* your faith in Christ every day have on your co-workers? your family? your friends?

❧ What can you do differently this week to help ensure that the people you encounter know that you believe in and follow Jesus?

Go Forward

Gather the group and debrief what people discovered while in pairs. Then discuss:

❧ Did you glimpse God in the face or actions of someone you saw worshipping him this week?

❧ How might your worship have been a God Sighting to someone this week?

Give everyone a sheet of paper and a pen. Ask people to write a letter to God, thanking him for who he is and what he's done in their lives. Close by allowing time for individual prayer. Play worship music, and give everyone the freedom to worship Christ however they prefer—sitting or kneeling, praying quietly, or singing. Encourage the group to spend the time thinking about Christ and worshipping him as the Lord of their lives.

Living in the Light

Before you gather:
You'll need a blindfold for each person. (Scarves, dish towels, head-bands, and bandannas all make good blindfolds.)

Learning to Experience God Every Day

Welcome everyone. Ask each person to tell about a God Sighting that happened this week.

Go!

After everyone has had a chance to share, ask people to form pairs and remove their shoes. Have them leave their partners and mingle with the group a bit before handing out the blindfolds. Then have people use blindfolds to cover their eyes completely. Tell people that, with their eyes covered, partners must find each other, find their shoes, and then help their partners put on their shoes.

When everyone has completed the task, let people remove the blindfolds and sit down. As a group, discuss what they experienced:

❧**How did it feel to be unable to see? What else made the task hard? What would have made it easier?**

❧**In what ways was communication between you and your partner affected?**

❧**WEEK 48—November 26–December 2**
Daniel 2:24–11:1; 1 Peter 4:7–1 John 3:6;
Psalms 119:81–121:8; Proverbs 28:15-28

❧How did you feel when you were able to take off your blindfold? How is this experience similar to walking in fellowship with others?

Go Deeper

Ask a volunteer to read 1 John 1:7. Have people form pairs to discuss:

❧The verse we just read says if we live in the light, as God is in the light, then we will have fellowship with one another. When have you found yourself living in darkness but still trying to have fellowship with others? What, if any, barriers did you experience? How did God get your attention?

Go Forward

Gather the group. Discuss:

❧How did you experience fellowship with God this week? In what ways did God communicate with you?

❧What will you do to continue living in God's light?

Close your time together by praying for each other and thanking God for who he is and the ways he communicates with us. Thank him for his light and the benefits of walking with him.

God's Precious Gift

Before you gather:
Set out a plant that needs watering. This activity will be more meaningful if the plant is "thirsty" for water. (Optional: Purchase a small plant for each person to take home as a reminder of God's gift of the Holy Spirit.)

Learning to Experience God Every Day

Welcome everyone. Ask each person to tell about a God Sighting that happened this week.

Go!

After everyone has had a chance to share, set out the potted plant and a pitcher of water. Pour the water over the plant until the soil is soaked and water begins seeping out the bottom. Ask a volunteer to read Joel 2:28-29. Have people form pairs and discuss:

❧How is this plant like our relationship with God and the water like the Holy Spirit?

❧What did God pour out on you this week? His love, mercy, or grace? Possibly his compassion?

❧**WEEK 49—December 3-9**

Daniel 11:2–Joel 3:21; 1 John 3:7–Revelation 1:20; Psalms 122–128; Proverbs 29:1-18

Go Deeper

Gather the group, and discuss:

❧How do you know when the Holy Spirit is active in your life? How do you discern the difference between coincidence and evidence of God at work? Explain.

❧In what ways have you seen the Holy Spirit changing you this year?

Go Forward

Have people return to their partners and brainstorm how they might pour out God's love on others this Christmas season.

❧What undeserved gift could you give this week? Forgiveness to a friend? Reaching out to a grumpy neighbor? Your time to help a single parent?

Gather the group, and encourage people to continue looking for ways to show God's love to those around them this week and all the weeks leading up to Christmas.

Ask people to look at the plant you watered earlier. As a group, ask God to saturate you with his Spirit, allowing you to pass along his love and joy to those around you.

Intimacy With God

....

Before you gather:

Purchase chocolate sandwich cookies, and scrape the filling out of enough cookies to have an unfilled cookie for each person. You'll also need one filled cookie per person. (Optional: Instead of buying sandwich cookies, make a batch of chocolate chip cookies. Prior to adding the chips, remove enough of the dough to make a cookie for each person. Add the chips to the remaining dough, and bake the cookies.)

....

Learning to Experience God Every Day

Welcome everyone. Ask each person to tell about a God Sighting that happened this week.

Go!

After everyone has had a chance to share, pass out the cookies without the filling, and ask a volunteer to read Micah 6:8 while people are enjoying their treat. Have everyone form pairs and discuss:

❧Tell about your best friend. What quality do you appreciate most about him or her?

❧Think about the cookie you just ate. What was missing? What would have made it better?

❧**Week 50—December 10-16**

Amos 1–Micah 7; Revelation 2–7;
Psalms 129–135; Proverbs 29:19–30:6

Go Deeper

Gather the group to discuss:

❧ **What one characteristic about God draws you to him most? Where did you see it this week?**

❧ **According to Micah 6:8, God requires us to do what's right, to love mercy, and to walk with him. Of those three requirements, where are you strongest? weakest? Give specific examples.**

Go Forward

After 10 minutes, gather the group. Pass around the cookies with the filling.

Say: **You could say our relationships with God are similar to our experience with these cookies. The first ones tasted OK, but something was lacking. A richness was missing. In the Bible, God has given us the recipe for rich, full, intimacy with him.**

Have everyone return to their partners. Ask:

❧ **Is your relationship with God just OK, or is it rich and fulfilling?**

❧ **What is missing from your relationship with God?**

❧ **What steps can you take to put that missing piece in place? What are you waiting for God to do?**

Call everyone together. As a group, thank God for the depth and richness of relationship we can have with him. Ask God to nourish your desire to know him better.

What Do You Really Want?

Before you gather:

Purchase a 2-inch flooring nail for each member of your group. Tie a piece of ⅛-inch-wide red ribbon to the top of each nail to make a Christmas tree ornament.

Learning to Experience God Every Day

Welcome everyone. Ask each person to tell about a God Sighting that happened this week.

Go!

After everyone has had a chance to share, have people form pairs and discuss:

❧What do you hope to receive for Christmas this year?

❧Tell about the most memorable Christmas gift you've ever received. Where is it now?

Go Deeper

Gather the group to discuss:

❧Think about the nonmaterial gifts God has given to you during the past few years. What did he give you this week?

❧**Week 51—December 17-23**

Nahum 1–Zechariah 5; Revelation 8–14;
Psalms 136–142; Proverbs 30:7-23

↬Think about the gifts you mentioned earlier. How do they compare to the gifts God has given you?

Go Forward

Ask for a volunteer to read Psalm 142:5; then have people form pairs to discuss:

↬In this passage, the psalmist says that God is all he really wants in life. If this were true of you, what would that look like? How would your life and the things you pursue change?

↬If you could ask God to give your child or best friend the most important gift he or she could receive, what would you ask for?

Bring people back together after 10 minutes, and encourage them to continue looking for God and his precious gifts in the coming week. Suggest that they call each other during the week to share how they've seen God during the Christmas holiday.

Begin passing out the ornaments made from nails. Say: **During this time of year, we remember Christ's miraculous birth and the amazing truth that God came to earth as a baby. Let this ornament remind you of the purpose of his coming. When you see this nail hanging on your tree, reflect on Christ's death, when he hung on another tree.**

As a group, thank God for Jesus' birth and his death, which allow us to live in God's presence for eternity. Ask God to continue revealing himself in significant ways to each person.

Blessings From God

....

Before you gather:

Go to persecution.com or christianfreedom.org, and print a story of someone who has experienced persecution for his or her faith. Have paper and pens available.

....

Learning to Experience God Every Day

Welcome everyone. Ask each person to tell about a God Sighting that happened this week.

Go!

After everyone has had a chance to share, ask a volunteer to read Revelation 21:6-7. Then have people spend five minutes creating a "Top 10" list of blessings they've received from God during this year of regular Bible reading. Ask people to form pairs.

❧**Share your list of blessings with your partner. What characteristic of God emerges most clearly from your list?**

While people are still in pairs, get their attention and read aloud the story you found on the Internet. Discuss:

❧**How is this person being blessed by God?**

❧**WEEK 52—December 24-31**

Zechariah 6–Malachi 4; Revelation 15–22;
Psalms 143–150; Proverbs 30:24–31:31

Go Deeper

After several minutes, gather the group and share insights from the pairs' discussions. As a group, discuss:

- Do you feel closest to God during trials or when things are going well? Why?

- Tell about a time when life was not going as you had planned. In retrospect, where do you see God? Do you see any purpose in the hardship you faced?

- Where did you see God's blessings this week?

Go Forward

Have everyone form pairs again to discuss:

- If you woke up one morning and found that everything—home, family, car, job—was taken away from you, would you still consider yourself blessed? Explain.

- What are some important blessings from God that you easily overlook?

Gather the group, and allow everyone time to share discoveries. Read Revelation 21:6-7 again, and as a group, thank God for calling you his children, for being your God, and for giving you the water of life. Ask God to draw each person closer to him in the coming year and to give all the group members eyes to see God at work in their lives.

After praying, encourage people to reflect upon their lists of blessings stemming from reading the Bible regularly throughout the year. Encourage them to begin again!

For more great small group resources, go to group.com.

Some Promises From God

God will always love you (Romans 8:35-39).

God will always forgive you (1 John 1:9).

God will provide direction for your life (Proverbs 3:5-6).

God will hear and answer your prayers (Proverbs 15:29 and 1 John 5:14).

God will always be with you (Isaiah 41:10 and Matthew 28:20).

God will enable you to face temptation (1 Corinthians 10:13).

God will meet your needs (Matthew 6:25-33).

Mind Challenge

You are trapped in a room with two doors.
One leads to certain death, and the other leads to freedom.
You don't know which is which.

There are two people guarding the doors.
You can choose one door,
and then you must go through it.

You may ask either guard one question.
The problem is, one guard always tells the truth
and the other always lies.
You don't know which is which.

What is the right question to ask?

Mind Challenge

You are trapped in a room with two doors.
One leads to certain death, and the other leads to freedom.
You don't know which is which.

There are two people guarding the doors.
You can choose one door,
and then you must go through it.

You may ask either guard one question.
The problem is, one guard always tells the truth
and the other always lies.
You don't know which is which.

What is the right question to ask?

More Promises From God About...

anxiety . . . . Philippians 46-7

brokenheartedness . . . . . . Psalm 34:18-19

death . . . . Romans 8:10

discontent . . . . Hebrews 13:5

discouragement . . . . Psalm 34:18

doing the right thing . . . Psalm 84:11

failure . . . . Psalm 37:23-24

fear . . . . Isaiah 41:10

God's discipline . . . . Proverbs 3:12

God's love . . . . Romans 8:38-39

guidance . . . . Psalm 48:14

guilt . . . . Psalm 103:12

hardheartedness . . . . Ezekiel 36:26

money . . . . Matthew 6:31-33

mourning . . . . Matthew 5:4

needs . . . . Matthew 6:32-33

protection . . . . Psalm 91:1-4

provision . . . . Matthew 6:28-30

sickness . . . . Psalm 73:26

sinful desires . . . . 2 Peter 1:4

sin . . . . Romans 6:14

temptation . . . . 1 Corinthians 10:13

troubled times . . . . Nahum 1:7

weakness . . . . 2 Corinthians 12:9

weariness . . . . Psalm 73:26

Treasure Hunt Clues

Clue **1**

People come, and people go,

Push me, pull me…who's to know?

Look up, look down, look all around,

But do not look upon the ground.

Clue **2**

I might be red,

I might be blue,

Gold, silver,

Old, or new.

Take me where you want to go,

But do be careful in the snow!

Clue **3**

I have four legs,

And you have two.

So when you're weary,

I can hold you.

Experience God Sightings™ with
The One Year Bible

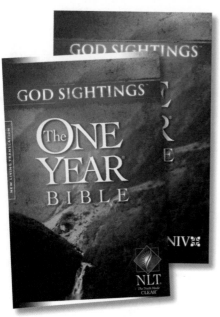

You have
*God Sightings: The
One Year Small Group
Leader Guide*

— now get the Bible that
will help you learn to
experience God every da

Find understanding and lasting inspiration with *God Sightings: The One Year Bi*
which makes Bible reading inviting, rewarding, and doable. Every day there's a
excerpt from the Old Testament, New Testament, Psalms, and Proverbs.

Use *God Sightings: The One Year Bible* to dive into Scripture and discover how G
is moving in your life. Together with *God Sightings: The One Year Companion Gu*
and *God Sightings: The One Year Small Group Leader Guide*, it will give you a new
way of seeing the world—and you'll never be the same.

Available in the New Living Translation and New International Ver

TYNDALE

Group

The ONE
YEAR
BIBLE

NLT   ISBN 978-1-4143-34
NIV   ISBN 978-1-4143-34